Savoring
SAGE TIME

Savoring SAGE TIME

The Journey from No One
to Wise One

I. Leahanna Young

iUniverse, Inc.
Bloomington

Savoring Sage Time
The Journey from No One to Wise One

Copyright © 2012 by I. Leahanna Young.

All rights reserved. No part of this book may be used or reproduced by any means, graphic, electronic, or mechanical, including photocopying, recording, taping or by any information storage retrieval system without the written permission of the publisher except in the case of brief quotations embodied in critical articles and reviews.

Limit of Liability/Disclaimer of Warranty. While the author has used her best efforts in preparing this book, she makes no represenatation or warranty with respect to accuracy or completeness of the contents or fitness for a particular purpose. The advice and strategies contained here in may not be suitable for for your situation.

iUniverse books may be ordered through booksellers or by contacting:

iUniverse
1663 Liberty Drive
Bloomington, IN 47403
www.iuniverse.com
1-800-Authors (1-800-288-4677)

Because of the dynamic nature of the Internet, any web addresses or links contained in this book may have changed since publication and may no longer be valid. The views expressed in this work are solely those of the author and do not necessarily reflect the views of the publisher, and the publisher hereby disclaims any responsibility for them.

Any people depicted in stock imagery provided by Thinkstock are models, and such images are being used for illustrative purposes only.
Certain stock imagery © Thinkstock.

ISBN: 978-1-4759-5757-0 (sc)
ISBN: 978-1-4759-5759-4 (hc)
ISBN: 978-1-4759-5758-7 (ebk)

Library of Congress Control Number: 2012920566

Printed in the United States of America

iUniverse rev. date: 11/07/2012

Wisdom is the use of knowledge, intelligence, intuition, and compassion to make appropriate choices.

Dr. Oscar Emerson Capps, PhD, LPC

For my loving sons, Darrell L. Young and Shaun D. Young

Because of your birth into my life,
I came to know unconditional love.

For my grandchildren and great-grandchildren,
who keep me living in happy wonder.

For all my families, those of blood and those
of choice who nurture the best in me..

Contents

List of Illustrations xi
Preface.. xiii
Acknowledgments xvii
Introduction.. 1
Accept Gifts of the Sage... 7
Time as Treasure 13
Dorothy, Astrological Sage 18
Accumulate Graces on Flights in Time 26
Get Right Side Up from Upside Down............................... 32
Arthur, the Bounce-Back Sage 38
The Blocks to Maturity 45
Living an Attitude of Gratitude 49
Nancylee, Ranch Boss Sage... 53
Build Balance into Life 58
Enjoy the Mystery of Life's Journey 61
Yolanda, Sage of Reconciliation 65
Critique the Critic... 70
Vicki, Learner Sage.. 74
Sage or Sourpuss, Your Choice: Using Our Power to Choose...... 80
Martin "Old Eagle," Native Wisdom Sage........................... 83
Segue into a Sage: Avoid the Slip into Senility 89
Sages in Disguise 98
Smokey, Sage on a Motorcycle.. 101
Connect with Change: The Twain Can Meet 103
Nancy, the Teaching Sage 107
Wisdom of Full Presence 111

Kate, the Serving Sage	114
Courage to Live on the Edge	123
Jean, Sage of Many Learnings	127
Afterword	133
Endnotes	135

List of Illustrations

Book cover design courtesy of Brent Benjamin Young

1. Reproduced by permission from Ashleigh Brilliant, *I Have Abandoned My Search for Truth and Am Now Looking for a Good Fantasy* (Santa Barbara, CA: Woodbridge Press Publishing Company, 1980), Potshot #641.

2. Photograph ("Baby Destin") courtesy of Brentleigh Lennon Young

3. Photograph ("Hands") courtesy of Brent Young

4. Photograph courtesy of Arthur Hall

5. Photograph (Nancylee Kennedy) Reproduced by permission from Jim Dirden (www.jimdirden.com)

6. Photograph Vicki Marsh

7. Photograph courtesy of John Aceti

8. Photograph of print courtesy Martin (Old Eagle) Hays

9. Photograph of Kate Roos with Storybook Club

10. Photograph of Kate Roos with Storybook Club reading book

Preface

Many travelers today use a GPS. On the journey from no one to wise one, it is helpful to know where you are now and what is ahead and be given alerts when you need to recalculate and make course corrections. *Savoring Sage Time* can be thought of as a kind of GPS to guide those who wish to continue to be of value in the world in their mature years.

We are living in a time in which a greater proportion of our society has years of life experience. As the baby boomers enter their wisdom years, we have the opportunity to become a culture of wise elders. Used wisely, this can benefit all. First of all, those with that experience must see it as a benefit that is theirs to offer.

People among us now have many years of life lived. Some complain of not being respected in this stage of life; others seem simply to resign themselves to the fact that reaching a certain age means being put on a shelf and seen of little value. Thankfully, there are those mature ones who continue their valiant journey. Those sages lead us to know that there continues to be value in our years lived.

The media's focus on the assumption that we should avoid growing old at all costs may create fear of approaching these mature years. Such fear may work as a way to sell products but does not give lasting peace and contentment. It is time to choose to honor who we are beyond how we look. We who have made a great part of the journey can only experience respect as we acknowledge and claim who we are now without regret or attempts to be where we have been already. Now is the time to gather the courage to stay consciously alive and aware. This is the time to feel enthusiasm for who we are and what we have to offer.

I. Leahanna Young

From my years as a mother, grandmother, and great-grandmother, I have had opportunities to observe the journeys of life's many stages from an up close and personal viewpoint. My passion for learning has privileged me to wear many hats:

- An educator and counselor of elementary through university students
- Grant writer to create an elementary counselor program, a gifted and talented program, and one to bring university classes on-site for the staff of the school district I served until my retirement in 1991
- Counselor for hospice patients and families
- Administor for a families and literacy organization
- Leader of people of different faiths, creating an interfaith group that met monthly to dialogue about issues concerning peace
- Member of the board of directors at Unity Church of the Hill Country, as well as the adult education ministry team, choir member, and teacher of adult and children's classes

Each of these hats allowed me various views of the human journey. Each has enriched my life and broadened my understanding and acceptance of many journeys.

I am informed by bachelor's, master's, and educational specialist degrees and years as a licensed professional counselor. I graduated from a continuing education program of study at Unity School of Christianity in 1995. Those years as student and teacher fuel my interest to research ideas and organize experiences to offer a kind of personal GPS. Use this to guide you toward the grand experience of sage with respect for self and fellow travelers.

Arun Gandhi, Mahatma Gandhi's grandson, said, "Respect and humility go together. Humility is not meekness, but the opposite of arrogance. A wise old Indian once said to me, 'Empty drums make the loudest noise.' . . . those with the least understanding are most arrogant."[1] As I interviewed living sages, many were surprised that anyone would view them as a sage. Given the invitation to be interviewed and share their life, most responded with hesitancy. "But I don't see myself as a sage or especially wise." I heard these words time and again from those I saw clearly in that wisdom realm. So what holds them back from their highest self? What keeps them from acknowledging all that a lifetime of experiences survived and lessons learned has brought? Is it that one quality of a sage is humility? Is it that our culture does not value or honor ones with these well-earned qualities and gifts to offer us? Is it a hidden fear of being nailed to a cross for being so radical as to tell truths others don't want to hear? Maybe a fear of rejection brought on by revealing their true stories? Is it our culture's marketing of youth and a negative attitude toward aging?

Whatever it may be, I am happy to say that what now awaits you within *Savoring Sage Time* are the stories of those who said yes to the invitation to be interviewed. At last, when offered the choice to have their story written anonymously, all chose to claim their own story.

They bless and entertain you with their wisdom, courage, sense of humor kept alive through life's difficulties, and, yes, humility. These modern day sages called forth what the Course in Miracles refers to in its Preface as that "little willingness" . . . the course emphasizes again and again is sufficient.[2] It touched me deeply to hear that just the invitation to be interviewed seemed to stir discussion among groups of friends of those with that willingness. Among their friends, they considered responses they wanted to make to topics to which I had asked them to give thought. Some reported their friends had similar reactions. Perhaps that was encouraging to some. At last, when the interviews were completed, a new awareness and appreciation was claimed for the lives they had lived and the courage the hard times had built. Many expressed gratitude for the teachers in their lives, the ones who had influenced and inspired them to become more than they imagined they could be, sometimes to be even more than family or others of authority had told them they had the potential to be.

As Joan Chittester said, "Every day we make our souls new again."[3]

ACKNOWLEDGMENTS

The birth of *Savoring Sage Time* began with an awareness of the sages who have contributed much to my life. By their example, I grew in wisdom. I acknowledge with gratitude all of them, those whose stories I was privileged to hear and record here and the many others I've known through my lifetime.

I want to express appreciation to a man whose name I do not know. I recall a two-hour job interview with a stranger. Instead of giving me a job, he gifted me with advice that changed the direction of my life as well as the lives of my children. It was a time in my life when I felt deeply concerned about how to provide for my young son and myself. I saw the only possibility was to abandon my last year of college and my part-time job in order to find full-time employment.

In response to a classified ad, I called to apply for a full-time job as a dental assistant. The doctor told me he didn't have time to interview me at his office. He instructed me to come to his house that evening. This sounded a little strange; however, a friend kept my son that evening. She agreed to come to the address I was given if I had not returned by nine o'clock. On my arrival in the privileged neighborhood, a welcoming lady opened the door. She escorted me into the den where her husband was waiting to interview me. Perhaps to put me at ease, she thoughtfully stayed during the interview.

When the dentist heard my response to why I wanted the job, he said, "You can never provide for your son as you want by working for what I can pay you as a dental assistant. You need to finish your last year to become a teacher."

Like a true sage, he outlined a plan for me. "Here is what you are going to do. First, see a friend of mine who will give you a job as a part-time dental assistant near your college. Second, save time you

I. Leahanna Young

are spending commuting by moving there. Next, apply for student financial aid. Last, do whatever is necessary to get that teaching degree."

I had never heard of student financial aid. He explained where to go and how to do this. I followed his plan and worked two part-time jobs. I went to school full time, studying after my son was asleep at night and on Sunday afternoons. The next spring, I graduated and signed a teaching contract.

In the midst of following his plan, I lost his contact information. I often regret that I never called to thank him for the rewarding benefits his sage guidance brought me. I hope that this acknowledgment will find him if fate allows and that he will recognize his act of kindness in Oklahoma City in 1962. I want him to know his belief in a young mother fueled her determination.

Months ago, I took a few chapters of this book, a lump of coal in my eyes, to my friend and editor, Donna Snow Robinson, to see if it was worthy of continuing my work and her time. She and her assistant, Jodette Weikel, chiseled and polished it until I began to see its possibilities. They patiently encouraged, inspired, and taught me as they gently held my feet to the fire to rewrite parts where they sensed I had more to say. My heart is full of gratitude for their skill, wisdom, insight, and patience.

Our mutual enjoyment of the game of mah-jongg brought Lizabeth Von Hagel into my life. She took my manuscript and, with her passion for punctuation and form, brought some clarity to this book. Lizabeth, I thank you.

Chris Bradley and I met at a Storyteller Circle here in Kerrville. Chris generously offered her editing skills that shed her own light on my writing even when she was in the midst of preparations for a month long trip. Another member of our Storyteller Circle, Dr. Kathleen Hudson, provided input that led me to see changes needed to improve readability.

A League of Women Voters meeting introduced me to Rhonda Wiley-Jones, a seasoned editor who graciously gave of her talent to polish and fine-tune my writing. She was yet another set of eyes to help me see better ways of expressing some ideas.

The generosity of writers has proven the truth of Hillary Clinton's wise reminder that "it takes a village." My heart is full of appreciation for each one of you. The many I may not have mentioned, please see your touch in *Savoring Sage Time* and feel my gratitude for your presence in my life. Each in your own way kept my passion for *Savoring Sage Time* alive during some of the tedious areas of detailed finishing this book required.

A masterful writing strategist, Leia Francisco, picked me up, dusted me off in a time of discouragement, and redirected me to continue writing. I owe the finishing of *Savoring Sage Time* to her kindness and skill.

My admiration continues to grow for the courage the sages I interviewed demonstrated. They struggled to tell their story with brave transparency. I saw them call forth new levels of fearlessness required of them to be so open and honest. I continue to hold a vision of developing such resolve in myself.

I wish to acknowledge several at iUniverse. George Nedeff, Sarah Bristow, and Mars Alma, you all at different times held my hand and gave your understanding for a first-time author. I say "Thank you" for your experience and expertise that kept me at work to offer a more readable book.

My family and friends were my constant cheerleaders. I can only say that, without you, I could not have continued to write. I especially express my gratitude for the artistic talent of my grandson, Brent Benjamin Young. Brent wisely offered the design for the cover of *Savoring Sage Time*. The soul-to-soul connection I've felt with him throughout his life seemed to instruct him even before I knew what was needed.

Most of all, I acknowledge the divine order of my life. No matter how many wrong paths I think I've taken, the perfect person or situation has been there to guide me back home to a place of peace.

To my dear friend Lana Slentz who stayed up all night proofing the galleys.

INTRODUCTION

We grow not older with years, but newer every day.[1]
Emily Dickinson

We don't grow old. We only feel old, and then others see us as old if we stop growing, learning, and connecting to our enthusiasm for life. The experience of being old depends on both our choices and our state of mind. Martin Buber said, "To be old can be glorious if one has not unlearned how to begin."[2]

Staying aware of the temptation to forget how to begin again allows us to resist getting stuck in a decade or, for some, a century. In 2012, some are still stuck in the last century, even trying to convince others that we should go backward rather than forward. Certainly there are values we will be well served to bring forward into this century. Sages know life is not about either—or choices. Wisdom knows how to think from a both—and view. When all we have to talk about is what has been, we become less interesting to be with, and we risk being labeled as old.

We are born a naked no one. Immediately we begin our journey of growing into someone special. Ideally, loving adults who see all the beauty, intelligence, and talents that only eyes of love can see surround us. At some point, when we have established an identity, we are ready to journey on beyond that identity. Our next task is to acknowledge that others also have their own talents, intelligence, and beauty, perhaps different from ours but of no more or less value. Then we feel a level of security within which is independent of the judgments of others. We no longer need to feel special. We can settle into the comfort of being nobody special again. This allows us to feel connected to all and immerses us into the wisdom of being everyone. That is our journey from no one to wise one. Though our bodies may age, our spirit will then feel the joy and freedom only a child can experience. We will have the eyes, ears, and will to see the world new every day.

You are opening an invitation to look at your life as a journey. What a trip. Not a race but a magnificent journey from beginning to wherever. You will meet people who are familiar and some who seem strange. Maybe you will discover some you have labeled as strangers are just unrecognized friends. Prepare for this trip by fastening your seat belt, tuning in all your senses, and opening your mind. Loosen your grip on fear and open your heart to a new experience of fullness of life.

In our history, both past and in the making, there have always been naysayers, the predictors of coming disasters. And always, in the present-day or ancient eras, we find sages (wise elders) offering a breath of fresh air, hope, and eyes to see the possible in the seemingly impossible. In these pages, I want to honor these wise ones and show the life they led and how they learned to savor their sage years.

In today's world of conflicting views, we often see only the chaos of despair and hopelessness. We forget that new creations beyond our present understanding can appear out of chaos. We need informed awareness and balance. We need to find the wisdom to move beyond this jungle of impossible choices into which we have stumbled.

In *Savoring Sage Time*, you will discover a map of growing from no one to wise one. The following are the ABCs of sage attitudes that you can use to carry you beyond possible distractions:

- **Awareness** allows you to notice the untapped gifts of sages. You can use these and combine them with the ingenuity of the young to build a better world for all.
- **Acceptance** relies on awareness without denial, submission, or judgment. Experience the freedom informed choice brings to acceptance.
- **Adaptation** is making conscious decisions about what is needed to move forward with integrity and respect for everyone.

- **Blocks** to forward movement are opportunities to build sage muscle. Each block recognized as such is a chance to empower us to overcome it. In removing each impediment identified, we grow in wisdom and strength. Acquiring the tools of the ABCs of the journey from no one to wise one strengthens you to continue your adventures with enthusiasm. You will hear the anecdotes and stories of others on the journey. They share their own experiences of overcoming blocks to maturation. Allow their life lessons to encourage you to see that even the seemingly impossible can be done.
- **Belief** in the wisdom deep within you requires introspection. Integrating outer knowledge, observation, and examples to enrich that inner wisdom is the work of becoming a sage.
- **Balance** is achieved by our awareness of overloading one part of our life at the expense of other parts we value. Developing routines to keep balance through consciously choosing our activities, friends, and commitments is a vital part of sage development.
- **Choices** made are one determinant of our present experience. A key to choosing wisely is awareness of the choices available. You'll see how those who choose from a both—and perspective are more inclusive. You will find how such inclusive views can inspire new connections of peaceful enjoyment of our sage years.
- **Change** is not about giving up or giving in. Change is about moving on. Advancing toward maturity requires the use of all of the ABCs and other letters of the alphabet. You will see the patterns of wise changes as well as the course corrections employed by the sages whose stories await you.
- **Connections** with those who are becoming wise permit you to see in them these steps being demonstrated. Ways of connecting the wisdom of the sage with the ingenuity of the young are found in this part of our journey. The value of using all the wisdom within and around you is revealed

in the stories of sages found along the way of this enlivening journey

Savoring Sage Time tells how to find life's gifts of taste, smell, hearing, touch, and sight by being fully awake and open in each moment. You can learn to be intentionally present to all of life, its highs and lows. You will also find the stories of others who are now experiencing such a life of being present. Some have reached this point through many years of living and countless lessons learned in those years. Others are enjoying being awake in their younger years. All offer a way to be alive in each moment. You will learn how to live fully alive without succumbing to the temptation to ruminate on the past or fear the future. This prepares us for all the riches waiting at the seeming end of the rainbow, a place we can enter called "Sagedom." From there, the sages lead us to cherish the ongoing journey with courage, humor, and anticipation.

Woven into *Savoring Sage Time*, you will discover the stories of ten sages who hesitantly agreed to tell me of their own journeys to sage time. May your adventure into these stories awaken in you a desire to prepare for or savor your own experience as sage, an appreciation for those who have done that courageous work, and a new respect for who you are now and can become. Here is your opportunity to see ways to mine the previously unnoticed unique wealth offered by the sage years. May you find in these pages a new wonder for this gift we call "life" in all its richness.

I invite you to grow with me as I write and you read, tasting, hearing, touching, smelling, and sensing the fullness of life. For in so doing, I now see that we prepare to enjoy this, the best of life for which the rest was made.

As Katharine Hepburn said, "Isn't life delicious?"[3]

Illustration 1

ACCEPT GIFTS OF THE SAGE

All worldly wisdom was once the ... heresy of some wise man.[1]
Henry David Thoreau

In order to accept the gifts of sages and incorporate them into our own journey, we need to be aware that they constantly present themselves as treasures. It is not unusual for these riches to be seen at first as problems. Our willingness to see beyond the problem to the opportunity in its hands allows it to be received as a gift.

"Savoring time with a plant?" This is a common response when someone hears this book's title. Even one of my doctors, when he asked what my book was to be called, responded with that question. Given he does seem quite young. Still, I've heard the same question from those in my own age category.

One of the advantages of the younger doctors is their seemingly love affair with high-tech medicine, a coin with two sides sometimes. However, this doctor makes great personal connections with patients. He sat beside me on his rolling stool and used his computer to pull up a dictionary to display the meaning of "sage" on the large screen of the examining room wall. He uses this screen to display each patient's picture and medical history for both doctor and patient to review. That did impress me.

All the while he was loading the dictionary onto the screen, he was commenting on how long it had been since he'd studied Latin, as though this was some ancient term. As soon as the meaning of sage, as a wise person of many years' experience, appeared on the screen, he sighed. "Ah, yes, now that does make sense."

Sages have this rare perspective of seeing where they are and where we as a culture are now. By being fully present to what is now, they may offer us their wisdom to see where our present choices are leading us. If we listen, we may use this to decide what is working to take us to where we want to go and what course corrections are needed.

When we are ready, sages will lead us to discover the value of wisdom and those who have acquired it. They can lead the way beyond our primary focus on money to experiencing a richer way to live. How often are young people encouraged to get an education to deepen their understanding of life, themselves, other people, and the world?

> ***Perhaps the time has come to see value in learning to live responsibly not just in learning to earn.***

One dictionary definition of sage includes a "profoundly wise person, philosopher, an experienced person respected for sound judgment."[2] How do we instill the use of sound judgment in children? Wise educators express frustration and sadness at an educational system where knowledge is offered on a temporary basis, that is, memorization of facts to pass a test to get a grade. They say the assumption seems to be, if given a storehouse of facts, students are educated for the use of sound judgment. Too often, we presume, if we tell someone, he or she should know it. In truth, we most often claim what we are told as our own when we prove it true by personal experience.

I hear sages asked, "Where in this educational system are young people taught to think, evaluate, and check facts? How do we best encourage the young to do what is required to allow wisdom of sound judgment to develop?"

Surely development of sound judgment is our children's greatest protection for staying free and being responsible citizens. Thinking for themselves can protect them against some enthusiastic, charismatic person creating unquestioning followers from wooing them. History reveals many dictators or charismatic zealots who have used such nonthinking followers to drink their Kool-Aid of death, as Jim Jones did.

A wise relative of mine says there is a difference between schooling young people to think as they are told to think and educating them to know how to think for themselves. Even our wise military leaders are realizing the need to train recruits to use sound judgment as well as respectful obedience to authority. These leaders are recognizing that both are essential for the personal survival of our servicemen and women as well as their others on the mission with them, perhaps even our national security. This sound judgment can protect us as a country from embarrassing actions that make us more enemies and less safe.

Joan Chittister writes, "Wisdom is not the quality of being wedded to the past. Wisdom is the capacity to be devoted to its ideals." Later, she adds, "It is the older generation that must turn the spotlight back on our best ideals, when the lights of the soul go dim."[3]

Another reference found in the dictionary under the topic of "sage" is to places, people, and organizations with the name "sage." You might see the word "sage" as elder, wise one, or whatever a specific culture uses to convey this meaning. Doug Meckelson began one organization that provides online sage wisdom. Doug is a man with a vision and appreciation for elders that showed up early in his life. His website, www.ElderWisdomCircle.org.is a treasure house of wisdom available at our fingertips. Here volunteer elders are available to respond to a wide range of questions. When should I talk with my child about sex? Should I accept a secure job even if it isn't my passion? How do I maintain a positive attitude as I grow older and face new obstacles?

Doug Meckelson and Diane Haithman have compiled some of the interactions of those in this circle into a book, *Elder Wisdom Circle Guide for A Meaningful Life.*[4] In their book, you find a list of traits of an elder: humor, action, love, listening, curiosity, perseverance, patience, goals, tolerance, family, spirituality, charity, hope, and attitude. Each trait is explored in the book, an inspiring, worthwhile read. The website also offers applications for volunteering to become part of this circle.

"One definition of wisdom I like," says Jimmy Carter, "is the ability to exercise good judgment about important, but uncertain matters in life."[5] How desperately is that good judgment needed in today's world, where the nightly news seems so filled with stories of those who clearly lack this vital capacity?

Elders of today sometimes express frustrations at feeling devalued in their families. They can be heard to say, "I seem to be of little interest to my children or grandchildren. I wonder if they think I have nothing worthy of their busy lives' time and attention. Their focus on acquiring more and more things, experiences, and excitement makes quality time with them difficult. This becomes more problematic as my body asks me to slow down. Keeping pace with them becomes more taxing physically."

I have noticed the elders I personally desire to give my time and respect are those willing to acknowledge the valuable lessons learned from their mistakes. They have stories that I sense are real and worthy of my attention. I recognize as I mature that quality times happen when the sharing of stories involves listening on the part of both the young and the elder. Our number of years does not entitle us to the spotlight of solo performance on the stage of time spent with others.

It is heartening to hear some elders acknowledge a desire to hear the stories of the young, a chance to learn from this younger generation how to live more easily in a fast-paced world of today. One key to facilitating this is to ask timely questions that require answers beyond yes or no. These sages know learning is a two-way conversation, never a sermon meant to straighten out another or turn back time. A statement such as, "Would you be willing to help me understand by telling me about . . . ?" can be a conversation starter. It acknowledges there are things the young know that I am ready to learn.

Barry Barkan, in his article "Culture of Change in Long-Term Care, Part I," gives the live oak definition of an elder. "An elder is a person whose work it is to synthesize wisdom from long life experience and formulate this into a legacy for future generations."[6]

Respect has come to me more readily when I am patient and undemanding rather than sulking and complaining. (I tried demanding. It didn't work for me.) As I express understanding and compassion for their fast-paced lives and detach from my sense of entitlement to respect, it sometimes comes unbidden.

A technique I learned through nonviolent communication is to make a specific request that reveals both my need to be connected and their need to stay up to speed. When I'd once driven a long distance to see two grandsons, I used this tool with benefit. I was sitting between these two teenage boys on the couch while they played with their Wii.

I watched quietly for a while, put a hand on the knee of each, and said, "Guys, I drove a long way because I need some time to visit with you. Would you be willing to finish this game and give me twenty minutes of your time?"

To my delight, they honored my request and finished their game as I watched. Then they even gathered the rest of the family around the dining room table for some honest catch-up on each one's life.

Researchers seem to agree that elders hold many gifts for us. However, William H. Thomas, MD, in *What Are Old People For*, laments the concept that we live in a time and place that allows older people to disappear from view. Dr. Thomas discusses how storytelling often communicates the wisdom of elders[6].

Such was the Native American way of passing on wisdom before some tribes even had a written language. Native Americans have told me of memories of adults gathering the children around and saying to a tribal elder, "Tell us a story about . . ." Often animals would be the central characters. As parents realized how this story heard as a child had led to wisdom in their own lives, they were motivated to call their children together to hear it. How often now do we hear parents or adults facilitate such learning for their children? This calling together around an elder acknowledges the parent's respect for the sage, thus setting a powerful learning example for the young.

Another Use of the Word "Sage"

The dictionary also defines sage as a plant. Many Native Americans hold the sage plant as sacred because of its purifying energies. They believe it heals by bringing the patient back into balance, cleansing the body and mind of negative thoughts and impurities. Sage played an integral part in ancient ceremonies. Those open-minded ones who may have no Native American blood have adopted it for cleansing today.

There is much information available online about one use of sage called smudging. Here a flame is held to a bundle of sage until smoke begins. Then the smoke is guided by a large feather or fan around the body of the participant who turns slowly to receive this blessing. Nearly anyone who wishes to relieve his or her worries, open his or her mind, clear negative thoughts and feelings, harmonize the body, and de-stress the spirit can perform this ceremony. It is a way to center on an intention when beginning an activity or facing a difficulty.

The use of the sage plant for such purposes may hold no interest for you. However, more people in health delivery systems are recognizing the wisdom power of the mind over the body. Research reveals the greater connection of body, mind, and spirit that many patients and health-care providers have realized. Using this connection in line with personal, cultural, and spiritual beliefs is beneficial as patients seek greater input to their health care.

Surely it is time to reclaim this term "sage" and all its meanings as it applies to the wise among us, as well as an herb known to the ancient ones for its healing.

Time as Treasure

The most costly thing in the world is impatience.
Harold (Jack) Dempsey (a sage in a local study group
of A Course in Miracles,)

Be aware of the words you use to describe your own concept of time. Hear yourself say, "There is no time to waste." Maybe to yourself inside your head, you hear a little voice saying, "They are just wasting my time." Hear statements such as, "I have some time to kill." All these give us clues to our own view of time.

A perspective of time encourages us to savor it. This view of time is free of judgment. The words "waste" and "kill" are not used in this view. This concept of time carries with it our intention to be fully present to each moment with all our senses open.

"Can time be tasted? Smelled? Touched? Seen? Heard?" one may say.

"Surely not," someone else may reply.

"Oh, yes, of course," you may answer. "Remember the smell of freshly baked bread coming hot from the oven that holiday long ago. Experience the warmth and safety reaching you today. Recall being in Grandma's kitchen that year, watching as she worked her food magic without need of recipe. Can't you still hear echoes of the stories told and laughter they triggered in us as we sat around Grandma's table, relishing that scrumptious feast we shared?"

Sit a moment, and let such scenes, sounds, smells, and feelings float to the top of your own memory bank. Bask in the glow of such gifts of sensation that savoring them brings. Be aware of how often invitations to trips down memory lane begin with. Remember the time when.

"It is not by muscle, speed, or physical dexterity that great things are achieved," Cicero wrote, "but by reflection."[1] How deprived is a culture that allows little time and space for such reflection.

How rare to find that place that offers only the gentle sounds of nature or perfect stillness that facilitate such savoring of life, past and present. Where do you go to find that quiet time to acknowledge all the gifts of past and present? When do you consider your own part in disappointments and hurts that permits you to see how to choose differently next time?

Learning the lessons of life's experiences may include mourning mistakes or losses as well as celebrating the gains. These actions require a time-out to reflect, to savor. Instead, we too often find ourselves rushing on to the next experience, perhaps to either forget the loss, thereby missing its lessons. We will never realize the surprising gifts of maturing and release that come with the willingness to do the work of grieving if we avoid giving the time to complete this valuable process.

The obsession to gain more and more things to feed a demanding ego in the driver's seat of our life is exhausting. The ego's need to prove our own worth drives us on with no time to encounter the satisfaction of growth opportunities of a life fully lived. Joseph Campbell offers food for thought about the value of a time out when he observes, "Where you stumble and fall, there you will find gold."[2] Reflection is the tool for noticing the gold.

I came to love the word "savor" as a result of an instruction given by trainers Jim and Jori Manske, who taught a process called nonviolent or compassionate communication. This new learning had a strong impact on the participants. We were eager to go out to share it with others. Jim and Jori had the wisdom to caution us, "Take time to savor this for a while. Continue to take in what you have learned. Let it be integrated into your own being and understanding. Only then will you begin to be the example out of which effective teaching is offered."

If you are interested in learning more of Jim and Jori's teachings on compassionate communication, see www.radicalcompassion.com.

I took the teachings and went for a sunset walk of Tranquility Island. There in the quiet beauty and stillness, I realized the power of savoring as a way of continuing and deepening learning beyond a classroom, a teacher, or an event. I felt myself dancing in the joy of this teaching, which had great value to me, whether or not anyone shared my excitement for it. I needed to convince no one of its value in order to claim it for myself.

From such savoring of the richness of each experience, we come to know Cicero's truth, as Joan Chittester phrases it when she says, "Cicero was right. The older generation has a great deal to give the world. But first, they must come to value it themselves."[3]

How can we fully value that upon which we have never reflected? How can we mine its riches from which true wisdom evolves?

Pablo Picasso said, "It takes a long time to become young."[4] I say it takes both time and time-out for savoring along the way to return to the carefree spirit of the young. That is a spirit so real, so genuine, that it finds amusement in such simple things as nature's wonders. That self can know both the tears of joy and express a wide range of emotions without false modesty or embarrassment.

The Native American culture has much to teach us about true time. We are free to use this time without judgments. Flossie Mathews, a teacher of time for me, is a friend from that culture. As the administrator of a Native American education program designed to offer guidance and counseling to students, I worked closely with the parent committee of Native American students. The committee and I shared the responsibility for seeing that their children's needs were served. Our first meeting was set for seven o'clock at night. I arrived early to be sure the room was ready and to greet the parents. Slowly, parent members of the committee began to arrive. Flossie kept assuring me it was not time to start yet as the time kept passing.

Finally at seven thirty, she said, "Now, it is time."

"How do you know?" I asked.

She replied, "Everyone is here."

What a concept for those of us who measure time by the clock, whether everyone needed for decision making is present or not.

I. Leahanna Young

This bond we have formed with the clock can rob us of precious passing moments we could use to connect. Instead, we become more tense and impatient. Notice how tempted we are to judge and label people who have a different approach to time. Consider the possibility of using every moment as a chance to connect. You may choose to just breathe a deep breath and connect with yourself. Check in with your body to see if it is hungry, angry, lonely, or tired, or HALT. Twelve-step work uses this acronym to remind us that we must honor our body's needs to live healthy lives. Connect with nature or someone near you. Being fully present by activating our curiosity opens our senses to experience the fullness of each moment in time. It provides a connection to yourself and all that is. Such connections bring peace instead of anxiety.

Become conscious of how you view this commodity we call time. Be aware that, in one sense, clock time is truly a human creation to measure life. We will be well served to be aware when it has become our master instead of our servant. The view we choose determines our ability to recognize our power to use it wisely.

Listen, every time you hear yourself say, "You know, I'd love to do that, and I do hope I can someday. Right now, I just don't have time," ask yourself if you've permitted time to become a tyrant, robbing you of conscious choice.

Time as Treasure

Sometimes you push me on
Hurry, hurry, don't be late
Then you drag by
Making me wait
No consistency in your passing
Speeding by or slow as molasses
Some fear the left behind
Others search to fill
With what they find.
One moment you rob of
Opportunity gone by

Savoring Sage Time

The next you curse with
Futures off in the sky
A miracle is now mine
A new understanding
Of timeless time
Old thinking only illusion
Mine now to assign my own conclusion
Each moment precious
Every breath sublime
Brings peace as I
Move in honor of Indian time

Illustration #2

Unspoken Love in Timeless Time

Dorothy, Astrological Sage

Our birth is but a sleep and a forgetting
The Soul that rises with us, our Life's Star
Hath had elsewhere its setting,
And cometh from afar
Not in entire forgetfulness.
And not in utter nakedness
But trailing clouds of glory do we come.[1]
Wordsworth

Dorothy is the first of ten living sages in my life you will meet in *Savoring Sage Time*. You will see in many a vision that formed itself early in their lives that led them to preservere toward a dream. In others, you will see how key sages in their lives redirected them to fulfill the role of sage by never giving up. Hearing and recording these stories confirms my belief that we all play a role not only in our lives but in the lives we touch along the way. We can choose to make a difference or miss opportunities to do so.

Reading has been a lifelong passion of mine. Our shared interest in books brought this sage into my life when I attended a book study group that met in her lovely home. For some time, I had no idea of her background in astrology. I occasionally read my horoscope and enjoyed it when it was encouraging and dismissed it when it wasn't. I had a skeptical attitude that was tinged with suspicion. When Dorothy offered to do the chart of anyone in our group who was interested, my curiosity overcame my suspicion, and I took her offer. She never attempted to predict precisely, but rather to say conditions indicated the possibilities. I have

> a friend, Hal, who shares my discomfort with those who use their sign as an excuse for not taking responsibility for their behavior. Hal believes we were all born under certain signs, which may influence our potentials. He thinks it is our responsibility to develop the potentials that serve others and us well and to overcome, as our life lessons, those which might bring harm. That makes sense to me, and in discussing this with Dorothy, I found she agreed. Her story reflects how she has done just that. I have found her determination to achieve a better life both intriguing and enriching to my own life.

The life of poverty into which I was born is beyond the imagination and compassion of many. It was not just financial, though at times that certainly led to and was a result of the real poverty. It was a poverty of education (with neither of my parents even having a high school education), self-confidence, resources, and examples of those whose lives were different. I lacked anyone close who could show me a way out of this poverty by recognizing my abilities and encouraging me. Those same factors kept my parents in the poverty into which they were born. At times, we survived on a meager diet with the occasional rabbit or squirrel. In my early years, neither of my parents knew what it was to be looked up to, only to be looked down upon.

Perhaps being the object of pity served to only isolate us more. I wonder if it built a kind of false pride that drove my father to drag his family from one town to another as he desperately did the work he could find in the oil fields. One year, I attended five different schools. I sometimes wonder if this desperation of little success in the midst of great effort and hard work led my father to turn to alcohol as a means of numbing out.

The year I learned to read felt like finding a key to a vision of a place where I could escape. That summer, the bookmobile came to our neighborhood every two weeks, and I was always the first in line. I took home as many books as I was allowed. As I read, I felt the wonders of access to another world, a world I somehow hoped might exist though I had never visited.

I. Leahanna Young

About that time, I had a friend, the preacher's daughter. Theirs was a little church where I found social asylum. In their home, I saw a piano and a family where the father came home every night. There the family gathered for hot meals. I was overwhelmed with envy for such riches and a desire to someday find that for myself somehow. The church, while giving me a social life, contributed nothing but greater shame and guilt to my young self. I tried to pray enough, to be good and unselfish enough, and to have enough faith that it might help me to gain that intangible life for which I longed. I carried these beliefs of not being good enough into my early adult life.

When World War II began, life for my family became a little easier for a while. My father spent a good part of those years building pipelines in Saudi Arabia. His employer sent a monthly allotment from his earnings, so there was a regular income. For the first time, my part-time job even supplied a few luxuries that helped to soothe my teenage ego.

Before the war ended, my father came home, and all that time-out from him ended. My need to escape became more intense as I saw him pin my mother against the wall with a knife at her throat and hurl accusations of infidelity at her. Even to my young eyes, I could see my mother was too fearful to ever leave the house. She barely spoke to anyone outside our family. I felt helpless, trapped by similar insults and accusations of being a whore, once just because a boy came to see me. I attempted to avoid my father's unpredictable behavior by not inviting the boy inside. Instead, I led him out in the yard to visit. We sat on the lawn and talked until my father noticed, and my hopes for escape from his rage were shattered.

He came barreling out the door, ordering me inside while shouting, "You little slut, you are just like your mother!"

I rushed inside, dissolving in embarrassment.

I now see my saving grace during that time was the attention I got from excelling academically and having my intelligence confirmed by my inclusion in the National Honor Society. That beginning of self-confidence, coupled with a spirit of determination to acquire an as yet undefined better life, drove me on. It rescued me over and over when my hoped-for protectors became painful problems instead.

I spent as much time as possible away from home, which was clearly a dangerous place for me. Graduation was only a year away, and then I'd be prepared to search for that intangible life of my dreams. In December 1948, that dream once again was interrupted. My father drowned on an outing away from home. We had no money, so Mother was offered a job as maid/babysitter. As the eldest, I knew I had to help provide for my mother and siblings. I went to work in a dime store. I became a part-time student, part-time breadwinner, and full-time big sister (all roles I would have to grow into).

The dime store where I found a job had a thirty-six-year-old manager who was separated from his wife. He fed my starving teenage mind with words I had longed to hear all my life.

"Dorothy, you are the smartest, hardest-working gal I've ever hired." Then after a while, he said, "You know you are very pretty. Would you like to go out with me to dinner?"

That dinner was unlike any I'd ever even known existed. It was what I now know as fine dining. This was followed by tender touches as well as gentle words, which I accepted with relish. The gifts and the word pictures he painted of a possible future together after his divorce were the next part of his enticement. I was more than willing to work overtime. No task was too difficult for me to take on. All I needed was to continue to hear from him all the loving words my father never said to me. There was nothing he asked of me I could deny him. Graduation neared, and my boss and treasured friend talked more and more of our future together. My intangible dream seemed almost within my grasp.

Then came a time when I most needed him, the reassurance of a wise, mature friend of good judgment. During that time of great need, I began to see the red flags showing his lack of true intimate friendship and support. I faced the situation alone and miraculously survived. Still, I needed that job and somehow wanted to believe he cared about me.

I completed my entry into the real world when my idolized "protector" and friend reconciled with his wife. My teenage illusions vanished. All my dreams for my future were shattered. The reality set in. It was up to me to protect and provide for myself.

Thankfully, I did graduate and began to prepare myself to become independent. My dream changed to becoming a businesswoman and my own protector. I pursued this dream until I decided to marry. It seemed the acceptable way to that better life that still seemed beyond my grasp. Even with my hard work, I still carried a belief I was not really good enough. Marriage was the path all females I knew were choosing, even my mother. So I married, experiencing yet another disillusionment, and after seven years, we divorced.

Five years passed, and I continued to hold on to my ideas of guilt and not being good enough. I allowed a young engineer in the Merchant Marines to seduce me. He was at sea part of the time. When he was home, it was party time, which was great fun and satisfying for a few years. Still a part of me knew there was more to life than this, and that marriage also ended.

I hadn't attended church for a number of years. I was restless and dissatisfied when a coworker gave me a booklet called *Daily Word* (the first key to the doorway of a new way of life). That little book of daily devotionals based on a whole new understanding of the Bible and all that is sacred led to my study of metaphysics. My lifelong beliefs about myself and the universe began to change.

In that study the messages came to me. "Everything in the universe is connected. I am created in the image of God. There is a spark of the divine in me."

I realized that what I longed for could not be found anywhere but within myself. Something inside me said, "What my life has been no longer fits. It is time for a new direction."

"But what?" I asked myself.

I had no plan for this new future. Surprisingly, the universe seemed to have a plan for me. A friend invited me to accompany her to visit an astrologer for a reading. I was fascinated with the information she offered me. I had always been interested in deepening my understanding of my own life, all my experiences that seemed beyond my planning, intentions, or explanation. Still I was skeptical until I began to see in her reading of my chart many of the answers I'd searched for so long. I realized I was already making a turn into living the future my chart showed.

At the end of the reading, she asked me, "Would you like to study astrology?"

With that question, she handed me yet another key to my new direction. She gave me the name of a correspondence course, and so my study of this ancient science began. I found myself studying with a group in an astrologer's office on Saturday mornings. The forecast in the daily paper was replaced with knowledge of the planets and what they were doing at the time in each person's life. My understanding of others and myself deepened, as did my confidence in a divine plan for my life and the gifts I came in with to fulfill that plan.

I was fifty years old, and a new life was before me. I discovered a new happiness. I directed it and my newfound self-understanding to my position at the M.D. Anderson Cancer Center. I was developing my career and planning my financial future. I no longer considered any male relationship necessary for my protection or provision of my happiness and well-being.

At last, I was free to enter into a healthy, deep, mutually respectful friendship with a man. We had different beliefs, which we each honored. Without marriage, that relationship lasted eighteen years. I always knew with certainty that I could count on him. As we walked together through some challenges life presented to him, I know he felt the same. He lived to be ninety years old, and our long, committed friendship and its rich memories has blessed me.

As I now pass my eightieth year, I have long and dear friendships with two cosmic sisters. These have taken us from middle age into our sage years. We give truthful opinions without judgments, and though separated by miles, hardly a day passes without our being in touch.

I. Leahanna Young

Cosmic Sisters

> Cosmic sisters,
> kin not by birth
> born to a kinship
> not of this earth
> kindred spirits
> meeting by chance
> brought together
> by circumstance
> bonded by knowing
> a likeness of mind
> sharing life's journey
> our lives entwined
> Cosmic sister
> did I know your face
> from some other time
> or somewhere in space?
> Dorothy Goudreau

My career and financial planning has afforded me a comfortable retirement in Kerrville. Here, I've made new friends and found a tranquil life through community and church activities. My now mature spiritual understanding has allowed me to contribute to two churches through the years. I know I have more to learn and something to offer.

Being in my sage years brings challenges, but also a certain freedom to choose what continues to enrich my life. I find here a new acceptance for my gray hair.

My mother, now widowed again, came to live with me. We spent many an evening on my patio, two women, both sages sharing our experiences, the hardships we survived, and the victories that brought us to this peaceful, safe, and comfortable time together. Her horizons had grown much wider when she learned to drive and graduated from cosmetology school in her fifties. She endured much, especially the heartbreak of losing her youngest son, my brother, toward the end of her life. She lived to the age of ninety-one.

    We are a generation that is now living longer, and there are more of us. I would like to see a change in the way our culture views its sages. We are a young nation that focuses on youth. Yet all around me, I see people in their wisdom years still contributing and making a difference in our world. Some are well known; others are ordinary citizens giving of their time and life experience as volunteers. In our media-savvy world, positive role models in television and entertainment could help with our culture's perception of those in these years of accumulated experience and wisdom with so much to offer.

Accumulate Graces on Flights in Time

Go out on a limb. That's where the fruit is.[1]
Jimmy Carter

Think of the gifts of grace that you have received or given during your lifetime—those moments of spontaneous acts of mercy, generosity, and love that surprised both giver and receiver, leaving both breathless with gratitude. As we bank those in our memory, we experience their indescribable dividends. We become more of what we bank in our minds and hearts. If we want to be more loving, we receive and bank love offered us. If we want to experience the forgiveness of others, we draw on the forgiveness we've received and banked in our memory to extend that. If we want an abundant life, we express gratitude for all we have in our present life as well as the memory of all we have been given. We can use these stored memory treasures to connect us to love in times when a disconnection seems inevitable. Such connections are acts of grace that depend only on our own willingness to open our hearts and minds. When we feel tempted to judge and shut down communication, we can open and offer forgiveness instead. We may need to let go of a fixed idea of judgment or hurt to draw on these treasures of restoring grace. We do always have a choice of whether to nurse the hurt or use grace to move beyond it. Out beyond emotional pain and blame, we find within us the grace that heals and restores. Grace is the gift that keeps on giving like a deposit that is guaranteed forever safe as long as we acknowledge its gifts and deposit them. Then draw on that grace to extend to others. You see, grace is an unending circle that flows easily unless we place a dam of fear or blame to block its cascade.

A post-Christmas flight back from Washington DC to my home in Texas took two remarkable turns. On this trip, December 29, 2006, I found myself in the middle seat, not my favorite. The lady on the aisle had a walker, and on the window side was a lady with a cane. They were both clearly my seniors.

I was just regaining my breath from the awe of takeoff. It always feels to me like participating in a grand miracle to be lifted within a man-made bird into flight. The window-side lady began talking. As I gradually tuned in, I realized she was casting aspersions on a person in public life for whom I have high regard.

"Don't you agree?" she asked, assuming I shared her view.

What to do? Ignore her? Shut down and turn away? This was to be a three-plus hour flight, which I did not want to spend either arguing or defending. I intended to use my time flying as a willing participant in this miraculous experience. Somehow it felt disrespectful to the miracle of flight to enter what could become a heated political discussion. I have found that people with strongly held opinions are rarely open to peaceful dialogue, which requires hearing another's point of view. So often, I leave a long flight feeling enriched by sharing the experience with another who might have begun as a stranger. I wanted a solution that honored my own needs and her attempt to connect with me.

Out of the glorious blue all around us, the answer came to me. I said nothing. Instead, I reached into my carry-on to search for a precious gift of a leather journal that my grandson gave me on my Christmas Eve birthday. Both ladies watched as I squirmed in the tight space, fumbling blindly before finding it. Then, having their attention, I introduced myself, and they followed suit.

Showing them my new journal, I invited, "This was a birthday gift from my grandson, who knows I write daily in a journal. I've never had a leather one before. It touched me that he knew the perfect gift for me. I'm wondering if you ladies would help me begin my entries by exploring a question that came to me this holiday."

They both showed interest and curiosity, so I continued, "I heard the phrase 'aging gracefully.' It set me to wondering exactly how people do that. I'd like to hear your ideas of how you are accomplishing aging gracefully. With your permission, I will write your comments in my new journal."

Wow! What a fast trip as we entered into this exploration, sharing thoughts and experiences. We found much common ground. The lady on my left shared my enjoyment of mah-jongg. Both shared some of the ridiculous experiences that aging bodies provide for our laughter instead of complaints. I came home with these musings.

Aging gracefully means:

- Being happy within yourself
- Staying in touch with what is alive within you
- Seeing the humor in the ridiculous
- Living beyond grief and anger to know joy again (both were widows)
- Learning to love what you thought was unlovable
- Accepting what you once thought was unacceptable
- Living with what is . . . without complaining
- Asking for what you need without making demands
- Seeing beauty all around you (the clouds were magnificent and provided quite a show along our way)
- Letting go of more and more
- Observing without judging
- Knowing how to return quickly to peace when upsets happen
- Living beyond appearances (spending less time looking in the mirror and more time looking within)
- Continuing to play, learn, and grow in mind and spirit

When the journal was filled at the end of that year, it was stored with those from previous years, tucked safely away since I began this journaling practice in 1988. Recently, it made its way back to my attention. Studying each of those ideas, I did a personal moral inventory check to see how I was doing with aging gracefully. It opened my mind to being more mindful of chances to nurture some of these areas.

I began to notice how resistant we are to accepting the gifts we are presented in this stage of life. The stage we discussed on that flight, which I, too, have now entered. Now I see we are encouraged to either try to ignore its arrival or focus only on our dread. Some complain of living in a changing body. We suddenly awaken to the reality that it is harder than ever before to deny that our bodies are forever changing. Whether we ignore or try to deny, by searching for that illusive fountain of eternal youth, we miss the grand adventure that stretches out before us. We blind ourselves to the joy of knowing the freedom that is ours in being our authentic selves. Letting go of concerns about judgments others make about our behavior or appearance frees us. We discover the escape hatch to choose what is comfortable in the midst of some wild style that passes quickly. We are liberated to truly know ourselves, to finally practice Shakespeare's advice: "This above all: to thine own self be true / and it must follow as night follows day, Thou canst not then be false to any man."[2]

I am grateful that, when it came time for me to savor my own journey into the sage years, that one and only leather-bound journal containing those gems from that flight was there, waiting for me to help me begin. After my personal inventory, I wanted a way to pass on these gifts of sages that were mine. So I began *Savoring Sage Time* with my reflection on my own journey as well as those around me. Where have we been? What life experiences guide us beyond becoming old to becoming sages?

My next flight was back in time to remember when I noticed signs of aging on my own hands. During a winter retreat I spent alone on Possum Kingdom Lake in Northwest Texas, two of my grandsons came to visit me on their spring break. One cloudy day, we sat looking out at the lake. I felt my oldest grandson's touch on my hand. That gentle touch flew me back through the years to a memory of a similar experience I'd had as a child with my own grandmother.

Life's Touch Connections
The innocent tracing of the bulging veins of my hand
Carries me backward through time.
I feel the sweet safety of my innocent own child self there in
the long ago.
I traced the bulging veins in Mam-Maw's hand,
Watching her vein roll slowly as my fingers pushed
this way and that,
Observing the slender, brown, spotted hands with
skin-translucent thin,
Marveling as I glanced from my child hand unmarked by time
To hers transformed by years.
Long ago, her fragile loving hands were laid to final rest.
Still, the skin-to-kin connection here calls forth
Tactile memories to comfort me.
I see again her hands' loving surrender to my touch,
Free of embarrassment about the marks of age,
No running for creams or salves to erase them.
Only complete surrender to that sacred moment,
No complaints or urgent business calling them away,
Her hands hemming my dress in time for special happenings
Her hands baking my favorite things,
Keeping them warm for my arrival.

Silently, my grandson Brent and I observe my hands and his. He listens as I speak to him of those beloved times with one he never knew. My hands now, with marks of age becoming familiar to me, connect us both back to a child who felt a similar sweet caress of unhurried attention.

Savoring Sage Time

Illustration #3

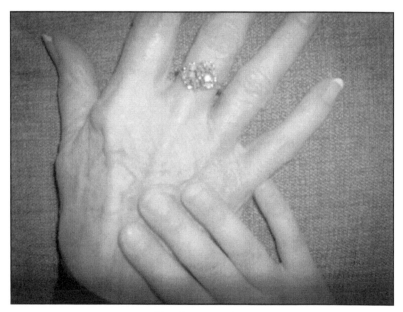

Hands across time

Get Right Side Up from Upside Down

*Our greatest glory is not in never
falling but in rising every time we fall.*[1]
Confucius

How many times in our lifetime has it seemed our world turned upside down in a split second? We are faced with the unexpected. We feel totally surprised and unprepared, overwhelmed. What seemed reliable is no longer there, leaving us wondering, "What now?"

Here, the sage characteristics of acceptance and adaptation begin to form. This formation rests on an individual's willingness to change. As we hold loosely what is now, we can let go when necessary. Then we avoid a waste of time and energy and can regain some sense of new direction. Eventually, we even find grace in the acceptance and adaptation required to continue.

Life continues to offer its lessons to secure my own willingness to accept and adapt. It is human to resist at first, perhaps denying the need for change, even to hope for a miracle fix. Maybe something outside me will change, and the upside-down world will be magically righted. The time it takes to quit resisting is often the measure of the pain we experience in learning each lesson.

I found myself in such a dilemma. I was literally upside down just last night. I've experienced insomnia periodically in my life. It has been viewed as a curse. My body seems less forgiving when deprived of sleep. Also, it's the blessing of a mind that seems never to tire of playing with ideas. Such thoughts as:

- "I wonder what other meanings there are for that word."
- "Oh, I could write about that experience I had today."
- "I'd really like to learn more about this or that."

It excitedly travels on and on down one exciting rabbit trail after another. It even continues cavorting when my body is weary, though my mind is never bored.

A few years ago, I stumbled onto a seeming solution to keeping this mind asleep even while making my midnight trip to the bathroom, which seems commonplace for many sages. If I didn't turn on any lights or totally open my eyes, I wouldn't fully awaken that playful mind. Kind of like, "Careful! You'll wake the baby." This made falling back into sleep much easier. For years, it worked well.

Then last night, my plan failed. I made it safely to the bathroom, even less awake than on previous trips, including half or less open eyes. Arriving in the right place is half the trip, right? Well, only if you sit in the right place upon arrival. Last night, I mistakenly miscalculated, going beyond my usual stopping point, and sat on the edge of the bathtub instead of the commode. This brought the shower curtain tumbling down on top of me, plastic liner along with the outside decorative curtain, rods and all. This, of course, startled me into a sudden state of wakefulness as I fell backward and sideways into the tub. There I was, not four on the floor, but folded in half four in the air wrapped in shower curtains and tangled in two rods.

Checking carefully, I thought, "Oh, good! No serious injury, not even to my pride because no one saw. Okay. Nothing broken. Only a slight pain on the back of my head from its sudden landing on the far edge of the tub and throbbing on the top of my head from the thumping of the shower rods."

However, I was still in this quite awkward position, mostly in the tub sideways with legs and arms straight up and tangled in shower curtain and its rod. In my mind, I could see myself as a human turned-over turtle. What to do?

"Empty condo on one side. Neighbor on other side on vacation. No use to yell. Hmmm. Wasn't there a story about God sending a rowboat, motorboat, and helicopter to rescue a guy on a roof in a flood? Is there a rescue team for human turned-over turtles in bathtubs, tangled up in the curtains and rods? It's worth a try."

I was ever so patiently praying and waiting not so patiently. I no longer needed to pee. I just needed dry jammies and a dry warm bed, if only the rescue team would hurry.

"Hmm, guess it's up to me," I finally thought.

Once again, I began the wrestling match with curtain and its rods, all the while conscious of knees I really wanted to protect from hard surfaces. My doctor said my knees each have one hundred thousand miles and I needed new ones. Finally, I became still and decided to approach the problem more gently. I slowly untangled myself, maneuvered out of the tub, found dry jammies, and fell back into bed. My knees were not too happy, but I was glad to be prone. I laid there trying to think of a new strategy. Somehow, after recovering from this adventure, I would develop one. Someday.

Sages waste little time in the regret of games of "poor me" or "if only." Instead, they put energy into developing new approaches.

Another characteristic of a wise one is the ability to use nondualistic thinking, a way of considering multiple views of any situation. We have been taught that up is good and down is bad. That is dualistic thinking. When we fall down, if we can manage to do it, we hop back up and look around to see if anyone saw us fall. If not, we breathe that sigh of relief that says, "Oh, good. Nobody noticed." If we need assistance, we sometimes insist we are all right, even before we check in with our body as if being all right erases the potential for embarrassment.

Richard Rohr, a Franciscan priest, has a different perspective. In *Falling Upward*, he challenges his readers to grow into the second half of life. He describes both dualist, the either—or approach, and nondualist as multiple views. With both views on board, those in the second half of spiritual life recognize and understand choices. The arrival at this broader view for experiencing the wholeness of life, he explains, is reached as we challenge our perspective.

We get to the whole by falling down into the messy parts—so many times, in fact, that we long and thirst for the wholeness and fullness of all things, including ourselves. I promise you this unified field is the only lasting meaning of up.[2]

PBS explores the unified field on *Nova*, "A Theory of Everything."

Einstein was simply ahead of his time . . . his dream of a unified theory . . . that everything at its most microscopic level consists of vibrating strands . . . string theory . . . encompassing all forces.[3]

In everyday language, the unified field is a psychological/scientific term describing what some call the big picture. In the unified field, all parts are considered important to the whole. Twelve-step work commonly uses the term "hitting bottom" to refer to falling down into the messy parts. Sadly, many of us have to keep falling down until we do reach finally that desire to be whole and to surrender all it takes to know peace.

A recent post on an inspiring blog, Martha's Blog (www.marthaobrien.com), offers encouragement to get right side up after a fall by noticing the view on the way back up again. The post, "Aliveness,"[4] is a contribution from a woman of years and wisdom. When we allow the fall and our recovery from it to be our teacher, it brings greater appreciation for many everyday routines. Martha O'Brien is a life coach. In my eyes, she is an artist of life.

"Aliveness" describes an afternoon walk that resulted in a fall and a twisted ankle. The black-and-blue ankle changed the walk into a hobble and a need to sit and scoot backward rather than walk to an upstairs bedroom. The absence of the benefits of good sleep, digestion, and improved moods that the daily walk provided were an unexpected part of this upside-down experience. Even little things like slipping on shoes without pain were no longer taken for granted. Eckhart Tolle says, *"Face how it is and say, I can either accept it or make myself miserable."*[5]

After the ankle healed, she said that, in ordinary moments, the joy of her aliveness floods her. The gold she found in this fall brought an awareness that life is uncertain. Things happen. The fall and its aftermath actually raised a new desire to savor tiny moments of joy and relish the gift of aliveness. She was no longer trapped in the dualist good/bad but could be in acceptance of the both/and of the situation.

I. Leahanna Young

To mature emotionally and spiritually, we face the need to change some long-held ideas or lifetime habits. This time-out to reconsider has been called our dark night of the soul. It is a time of questioning what is really appropriate now so the journey can continue. Here is where we meet new truths or new views of old truths. It is common during this time to feel unsettled or even tense and at sea.

Our inner voice is saying, "I always thought this, but now that I look at it differently I think this . . . What am I to believe? I was told that, but my life experience tells me this . . . I see the exact opposite of the carved-in-stone idea of my childhood is true for me."

We may also say, "I see why I needed to believe or view it that way as a child, but as an adult, I see I have other choices. Now I see a broader view."

Whether the need to right ourselves is physical, mental, emotional, or spiritual, it has common experiences for all who become sages. A vital characteristic of all the sages I've known is they have known pain and some humiliation. All endure a period of questioning. Eventually though, they laugh and learn. They are able to stay somewhat unattached to what they believe to be true now, knowing there's even more to learn that may alter their present truth. Looking back, I see how being able to hold everything lightly has allowed my opinions and attitudes to change and nurture me toward my next transition, right side up again.

Windmills of Life

Winds of life
Buffet and blow.
Causing holy windmills
To turn in me.
Opening my ears to hear their whispers

Be still and listen

Breathe . . .
Open . . .
Lift.
Sink . . .
Settle . . .
Surrender.
Allowing me ever to know
No happenings by accident
No occurrence wasted
Only manna's daily bread
Eternally fed
For my soul to grow.

Arthur, the Bounce-Back Sage

Serenity is not the absence of conflict,
but the ability to cope with it.[1]

> Arthur Hall exhibits the need to get back up after finding himself upside down several times. You will read next of the courage and determination he calls forth to do that. Overcoming life situations, some of his own making it seems and others over which he had little say, he chose to retrive from them opportunities out of which sages are formed. Many such claimed opportunities were made possible because Arthur was willing to acknowledge he needed help, humble himself to ask, and heed advice given. Sage Arthur is an example of how sages are formed through the choices they make. The mistaken choices that are recognized, corrected, and learned from become the gold found where you stumble and fall of which Joseph Campbell speaks. Art's honesty and openness in his willingness to share both the stumble and gold are elements of many sages I have known.

My twin brother and I made our entry into this world on April 14, 1921. On April 14, history has recorded the assassination of President Lincoln and the sinking of the *Titanic*. Not an auspicious beginning.

The 1920s were boom years, and my father prospered. However, I never knew my mother as she suffered from mental illness and was confined to a mental institution from which she was never released. My brother and I, along with my older sister, were installed in private boarding schools and sent to summer camp in the off school months.

Savoring Sage Time

In 1931, my father married his secretary, and we all moved, except for my sister, from Boston to Los Angeles. My brother and I went by train, stopping in Iowa for a brief stay with an uncle. We made the whole trip by ourselves at the age of ten. My sister went to live with another uncle in Iowa.

After a year, trying to make a go of it in California, my father gave up, and we went back to Boston. It was February, and we were riding in the rumble seat of a Model A Ford. Needless to say, it was exceedingly cold.

The Great Depression had started. My father lost most of his accumulated wealth during the stock market crash of the late 1920s, and times were difficult. By this time, at the repeal of Prohibition, my father had taken up with alcohol and turned into a violent alcoholic. On more than one occasion, he was summoned to the school my brother and I attended, where he was asked to explain the bruises on our bodies. We delivered newspapers in the morning, rising at four in the morning, and again in the afternoon. Then we worked in a bowling alley setting up pins until eleven. It wasn't long before the local police in New London, Connecticut, where we lived, became used to us pedaling our bicycles after curfew.

At one point, I hitched my bike to the tail of a highway transport truck and rode to New Haven, some sixty miles distant. The police picked me up, and my father came to get me. All the way home, not a word was spoken between us. When we arrived home, I was confined under lock and key to a small room over the garage for several days.

Meanwhile, my father's drinking worsened. At last, it was May, and my brother and I managed to graduate from high school. Shortly after that, my brother disappeared, and I did not know where he was for more than two years. So I left as well, hitchhiking my way to Chicago, where I wandered the streets for four days without anything to eat. The juvenile authorities picked me up and put me in a welfare house with other indigents. One night, a psycho came after me and another inmate with a switchblade knife, and we both went out the window.

I. Leahanna Young

    We hopped a freight train and went to Louisiana, where the sheriff accosted us and locked us up. Being Yankees didn't help our cause. Folks in that area were still fighting the Civil War. After another period of confinement, we headed west via empty boxcars, sleeping in hobo jungles and knocking on back doors of houses for something to eat. When we arrived in Los Angeles, my buddy left to return to his family home in a suburb of Los Angeles, and I never saw him again.

    I turned myself in to the welfare program, and I was assigned the job of teaching English to the undocumented Mexicans who, even then, were swarming across the border. After a short stay, I was put on a passenger train and sent back to Boston. I then joined the Civil Conservation Corps (CCC) program and spent a year on the Canadian border in northern Vermont, where the temperature dropped to minus forty in the winter. While there, the secretary of the high school we had graduated from had located my brother, living in Philadelphia. When my year's enrollment in the CCC was up, I joined him there and was able to find employment until the war came along.

    My brother and I entered the army in September 1942, and we were sent to a training facility in Virginia. I had decided the war was going to last a while, so I'd do the best I could. An officer training school was located on the grounds, so after completing basic training and going through non-com school, my brother and I both applied for Officer Candidate School (OCS) and in due course were accepted. I received my second lieutenant's commission two days after my twenty-second birthday in April 1943.

    In January 1944, I sailed on the *Queen Mary* to Scotland. I spent the next several months on the southern coast of England training for the forthcoming invasion of Normandy. After wading ashore at Utah Beach, I participated in four battle campaigns, including the Battle of the Bulge, and I was among the advance American forces liberating Paris. After the war ended, I was transferred to Paris. I arrived on July 14, Bastille Day, the first free day of the greatest of French holidays since before the German occupation. It was a truly memorable occasion. I spent the final six months of my wartime activity as commanding officer of a company that had been stationed (in Paris) since the liberation.

It was cold in the Bulge and chaotic in both places. That is all I care to say. I learned not to pull up those memories for they still give me nightmares if I talk of them.

I had given my father's address to the army, and I was sent to Fort Devens in Massachusetts for separation in January 1946. I was returned to New York again on the *Queen Mary*, only this time in a straight line rather than the zigzagging, which had made me extremely seasick going over. Going over, the ship altered its course every seven seconds to avoid the U-boats. That would have been a prize for the enemy, as fifteen thousand soldiers were on board. One morning back in Boston, I woke up to see fourteen inches of snow on the ground and vividly remembered my ordeal in the Battle of the Bulge that produced frostbite. I wanted no more cold and ice, so with a wartime leftover used car I purchased, I drove across the country to San Francisco, where there was no snow. The car promptly died.

After a period of three years going from one fruitless job to another, I wound up as a traveling sales representative with a large steel company. At one time or another, I covered all of California from one hundred miles north of Los Angeles to the Oregon border. I did this for over seventeen years, spending much of my time alone in small backwoods localities and beginning to follow in my father's footsteps with alcohol as my companion.

Eventually, alcohol became my downfall, and I was unemployed. I had been through two failed marriages. I had no money or place to live. I had no means of transportation in an area that had no public transportation.

I turned myself in again, this time to AA. There, I met a man responsible for turning around my life. While my father rejected AA and died of a stroke caused by excessive drinking, I listened to what this man said, which basically was, "If you don't stop drinking, you'll die. You surrender unconditionally and accept the fact you can't handle alcohol or your warranty will run out in six months or less."

I. Leahanna Young

I hated this man, John. He was loud and outgoing. He seemed happy and gregarious, and I had a headache caused by a terrible hangover. Still, I listened and found great support and encouragement from him. I took comfort in his assurance that, if I stumbled, I was to just start over. That was almost forty-five years ago, and I haven't had a drop of alcohol since.

After eight months sober, my unemployment insurance was about to expire, so I went to a member of the cloth who had a record of success with alcoholics. He was a Pentecostal preacher, Brother Jim. He agreed to hear my fifth step, and I started telling him my story. He stopped me by saying he didn't need to know all that.

"Are you sorry for what you have done?" he asked.

I quickly answered, "Yes."

He told me, "Get on your knees, and tell God that."

I did.

Then he said, "God has forgiven you. Now you forgive yourself."

My second wife had lived in Hawaii for three years while her father, a naval officer, did a tour there. She used to talk about it, so I told Brother Jim about it and said I'd like to see it because I could find no suitable work in my present locality. He opened the Bible and read Matthew 6:25—34. (This series of verses starts in verse 25 with Jesus admonishing us to not worry about what we will eat or drink or wear. He describes how the birds of the air and the lilies of the field are cared for assuring us that surely we are as valuable as they. It ends in verse 34 with encouraging us not to worry about tomorrow.) When he was done, I went home, phoned United Airlines, and charged a one-way ticket to Honolulu. After I liquidated my worldly possessions, I had four hundred dollars to my name.

This was a major turning point of my life. During my twenty years in Hawaii, I became more than a wandering recovering alcoholic. I was deeply involved in AA and, as a result, wound up as chairman of AA's Intergroup, the primary one responsibility for the island of Oahu. When my term expired, I was reelected for a second year. I joined the YMCA and began a physical fitness program, including jogging four miles a day. I logged over twenty-five thousand miles in this endeavor. I secured a position with a small company with two sales representatives. One had given his notice the day I phoned seeking an interview. I went to work the following week and stayed almost twenty years until I retired. I taught a women's class in physical fitness two nights a week at the Y. This ended when I found my future wife. She saw the potential danger in being closely involved with so many attractive women. After we met, I quit that part-time job, and we were married. She took me to forty foreign countries as part of her work privileges. It was the happiest period of my life.

I also joined Toastmaster and, as area governor, participated in a series of speech competitions, which resulted in my selection as a contestant at the finals for the entire state of Hawaii two years in succession. When I retired, we moved to Junction, Texas, where my wife's sister and mother lived. She died there, and I moved to Kerrville, Texas.

This was a period of deep despair as I grieved my beloved. With the help and support I found here, I survived and even thrived again. I reunited with the Unity Church I'd so enjoyed in Hawaii by attending Unity Church of the Hill Country in Kerrville. I serve there as needed, including Sunday lesson bringer, worship assistant, and, most recently, usher.

Last year, I was given a free trip to Washington DC to visit the World War II Memorial as well as all the others located in our nation's capital. I was among thirty World War II veterans so honored. The Alamo Honor Flight program from San Antonio, who collected the money to fund our trip, sponsored us.

An elder who can certainly be called a sage whom I've always admired is Winston Churchill. His quote, "Never, never give up,"[2] has inspired my life.

Illustration #4

Bounce back sage

The Blocks to Maturity

My youngest son left home for college just as I entered my fifties. I often found myself emotional and restless, wondering if I should apply to become a foster parent.

I asked my doctor, "Am I entering menopause?"

He asked, "What has changed in your life?" With a smile, he so wisely said, "Don't do anything drastic. Just get on with your life by deciding what you want to do now. What have you postponed that this time makes possible? In a couple years, you will discover you are enjoying a new freedom and a new you."

The empty nest syndrome is a common ordeal for many. This is a time of a woman's life when new choices are possible. That doctor's wise advice ushered in a new phase of life. It opened new doors to walk through to a newfound self. Invitations to travel that I had dreamed of for years started coming through those opened doors. I became part of a group of coworkers who for years enjoyed a spring break trip to places beyond my dreams. I am thankful for that doctor's wisdom. He knew I needed a change of perspective, not a pill. That advice removed a block of being stuck in the identity as a parent. Seeing that phase completed moved me to the next life adventure, just as my sons were doing. I see how that freed all of us to grow toward a closer than ever relationship. This new connection of adult sons, now able to take charge of their own lives, to a mom who has an exciting life of her own allows us a chance to converse with new interests that enrich both.

Many obstacles keep some people stuck in one decade or a once-appropriate identity. When they are stuck, they block a willingness to continue their journey. Tools of understanding are needed to move beyond these blocks.

Keep Growing Up

It is common to get so caught up in one decade that we just want to stay there. One resistance to the responsibilities of growing toward adulthood has been referred to as the "Peter Pan syndrome" in men. These young men enjoy a mother stuck in her role of parent caring for or pampering them. However, some young adults look at parents stuck in the identity of parent as unwelcome distractions to their own completion of becoming adults.

Even mastering goals in our forties and savoring that sweet taste of success can block upward movement toward becoming a sage. Enjoying more and more rewards can cause us to fail to recognize when enough is enough. We may fail to notice that having more can also bring more fear of loss. Later, when faced with the possibility of retiring, we might say, "But I love my work and the people I work with. I just can't imagine life without this."

Faced with the choice of stopping something we love or venturing into the unknown of retirement and the unfortunate idea of doing nothing, it truly seems a no-brainer choice to make no move at all. We hesitate to leave that comfort zone of the career we've inhabited for so long. Our culture offers so little instruction in the valuable work of becoming a sage, which is perhaps the most rewarding of all our life's work.

Welcome Change

A spiritual leader whom I highly admire was once challenged that something he had just said contradicted a previous statement he had made many years before.

He responded confidently and peacefully, "I reserve the right to change my mind when I acquire new knowledge and experience."

Potential sages stop along life's way and ask themselves, if they are especially brave, "Could there be another way to see or experience this?"

Asking such questions may open doors to a deeper knowing of self and the God of our present understanding. This is often a far larger, more intimate God. [i]

Then there are those who try to hold on to grown children to avoid facing change. In my observation, that thief steals growth from both parent and child and withholds the joy of experiencing those relationships at an adult-to-adult level.

Release Attachments to Self-Image

It may be an attachment to a self-image that no longer fits. Susan Howatch, in her series of six novels called *The Starbridge Series*, refers to this image as "glittering images."[1] Sometimes we work so hard in one stage of our life to build such an image of ourselves that to imagine it being tarnished by revealing our shadow self becomes frightening. Still our spirit calls us to a deeper understanding and requires us to reach down into our depths for the courage to grow into bigger ideas of who we are. This work of grand surrender transforms us into those fun-to-be-with, transparent people with nothing to hide or fear. Franciscan Priest Richard Rohr, in his lectures on *A Spirituality for the Two Halves of Life*,[1] speaks of the importance of moving on into the second half. I observe that those who seem stuck in that first half of life rarely, if ever, experience a laughing God and seldom seem to laugh themselves.

Accept Responsibility

This can be a direct clash with the universal need for freedom. Those on the journey to being wise learn ways to be a responsible human being and to meet their need to be free. They discover saying no to one thing means saying yes to another. To say no in a style that acknowledges needs of all is a skill taught in nonviolent or compassion communication. Responsibility to be true to self can honor the needs of others.

The release of all blocks to maturity is essential to avoid skipping developmental tasks. To leave this task incomplete can rob one of that golden prize of sagedom. Overcoming our resistance to change and its responsibilities and going back to finish unfinished tasks allows us to move on through to the prize.

There is an awakening to the ongoing process of growing up. Most have become conscious that reaching the magic age of twenty-one is not accompanied by the title "adult" and all the hoped-for pleasures and freedoms of being a grown-up. That is actually what I expected, as I suspect many others did. I only experienced repeated disappointments and so much yet to be learned and completed.

More is being written about what this process of continued maturing looks like. Gail Sheehey has researched and written several books on this topic. Gail does a thorough research and reporting of adult developmental stages for women and men. My last favorite is New Passages, Mapping your Life Across Time. Having an abundance of sons, grandsons and great grandsons I find her insights into male developmental stages useful in understanding and supporting them in their developmental stages. Each time I found the courage and tools to respond to this inner call to go back and finish the previous decade's tasks, I realized rich rewards.

One vital tool for me was that of reflection. This tool has also given me insight to my reactions as a mother to my children and now grown grandchildren. By understanding and having done this work myself, I can applaud their determination to complete their tasks. I support them in whatever time that requires rather than judge them for not getting on with life quickly. For I know that, in so doing, they are prepared to continue growing beyond a time of needing that childhood parent to control their lives and make their decisions. Watching without judgment, as family and friends accomplish or resist each task, has taught me and moved me toward my own adulthood. Long ago, I heard a saying that the two greatest gifts a parent gives a child are roots and wings. I was blessed with parents that, as they grew, gave me both. Those gifts set me free to travel through the stages of life that have brought me into my own eighth decade.

LIVING AN ATTITUDE OF GRATITUDE

The real voyage of discovery consists not in seeking new landscapes, but in having new eyes.[1]
Marcel Proust

You must be the change you wish to see in the world.[2]
Mahatma Gandhi

To be fully present with open heart and mind to what is before us allows us to learn from it and offer to it something of lasting value. I have high admiration for Nelson Mandela's steadfastness as he remained true to the passion he felt for a free Africa during his time of imprisonment. He used his commitment to living in integrity with his truth to practice his belief in the right of everyone to be treated with respect. By his compassionate attention to those around him, whether they treated him with respect or not, he took responsibility for living out his commitment to treating others with respect. This commitment created within him a willingness to be present and become a transforming force in the life of his jailer. Nelson Mandela's life reflects how he consistently practices his beliefs with a quiet conviction that he is responsible for his actions only, not the reactions of anyone else.

Pollyanna was one of my favorite books as a child. I read it over and over. With each reading, my admiration grew stronger for the joy she felt and brought to others. No doubt, a part of my child mind adopted some of that into my being. I have often been accused of being too Pollyanna or seeing through rose-colored glasses. While it has led me to fall in love at times with what a friend calls eternal potential, even that left me with some happy memories after the tears dried.

Through the years, there have been many predicted disasters that never happened, such as Y2K. Living in an attitude of gratitude requires some healthy skepticism of those who claim they know for sure what is ahead. Certainly a wise person looks at information, checks facts, and takes responsibility for any change that he or she may be able to make to prevent real possible problems. Often, predicted, certain disaster will only become disaster if we resist needed change. Those who live in constant fear of impending doom are not much fun to claim as close friends. Those who deny all responsibility for their own contribution to perceived difficulties are simply living in denial. They could choose another perspective that would move them out of the victim role and into a sense of empowerment.

Those who spend much of their life energy focusing on the possible dangerous side effects risk losing the joy of the moment. We can so easily be distracted by what is simply passing by.

An ex-husband of mine used to say when I was driving, "Leahanna, focus on the road. Glance at the scenery."

He was right. That was a great gift he gave me. When too much time is spent only watching the scenery go by, the steering wheel of our life tends to follow our focus. Then we hear the thwack-thwack warning of the bumpy rides, "Danger leaving your lane" or "Look out! Going off the road."

If we live with a sense of fear or lack instead of gratitude, we can be distracted by trying to hang on to what we think is needed or good. We frequently need to get on with our own journey. A spiritual saying puts this succinctly, "Where attention goes, energy flows." Perhaps you have borne the pain of trying to hold on when it was time to let go. When you find yourself trying to hold on, making two lists is a great pain reliever:

- A list of all you are grateful for right in this moment in time
- A list of things you can do to enrich your life and/or the life of another

Our world seems full of potential threats in the news, conversations, emails, or even our entertainment world that is filled with violence. What a breath of fresh air is ours when we hear a story of gratitude expressed for a thoughtful act.

People who want to focus on and live in peace can be seduced by those in authority, who tell us, "It is okay to hope, but we must prepare for the worst." Living in gratitude raises a question of how much hoping one can do while focusing on preparing for the worst. Pollyanna seemed always able to find the best even in what others saw as the worst. She called it the glad game. This is not living in unawareness and ignoring what is happening around us. Rather, it means preparing ourselves by beginning each day with a commitment to see opportunities to be thankful, to be a presence of peace in the midst of whatever may happen in this day. Let that be your Plan A. If it seems wise to have a Plan B to address distractions from Plan A, develop that while keeping your focus on Plan A.

In *What are Old People For? How Elders Will Save the World*,[3] William H. Thomas points at our youth-obsessed culture, for which we pay a dear price of surrendering our faces to the war on wrinkles. We are being asked to unmake what we have spent a lifetime making. Dr. Thomas puts his finger on the exact loss we can feel as we acknowledge a maturing body without honoring the person inside. We can to be grateful it still breathes, supports life, and giggles and plays (even if primarily inside it's imagination). We can choose to resist the media temptation to look forever young. Instead, we can honor our years of life and the best of its experiences. We can change our language about who we are now. Instead of age spots, we can label them "wisdom spots," and wrinkles become "laugh lines." A slower pace lets us use all our senses to enjoy nature. Just these simple adjustments of our focus from resisting what is now to being thankful for the now that is. Eckhart Tolle expounds on this in *The Power of Now*.[4]

Elizabeth Kubler Ross goes so far as to view gratitude as a great power. In *Life Lessons*, she gives us food for thought in her idea that the grateful person is a powerful person. She even describes the fine art of gratitude as the source of happiness, power, and well-being.[5]

I. Leahanna Young

David Kesseler, the co-author of *Life Lessons*, talks of how he has learned much about living in gratitude from the dying as they taught him about the preciousness of life. We claim all we have been through that has delivered us to be all we have become. No longer are our (hospice) patients willing to settle for just being alive. They want to feel alive.[6] To be in the presence of those who can feel fully alive in the midst of a body that may be growing weaker inspires gratitude for that privilege.

My goal is to have my maturing body reflect my attitude of joy at having lived its years. I intend to not lose myself, even as I become who I am next to be.

There are those of us in these latter decades of our journey who dare to discover and claim our true self as we go along. We are no longer willing to pretend to be who we are not. We gather courage to be more or perhaps less than someone might expect. We say yes only when we mean yes. This requires us to know when being true to ourselves is an essential part of that decision. We consciously go back to complete developmental tasks left undone in previous decades.

In his book, Dr. Thomas tells of an African proverb that a friend, Bernard Mambo, who grew up on the Ivory Coast, shared with him. "Losing an elder is like the loss of a library."

We who have lived and even grown through the disasters of life can live these years in integrity. We give thanks for those who have molded us into the sages of today. Living authentically with regard for all will bring a balance of hope and sanity into a seemingly insane world.

In a quote from Virginia Ironside's book, *Your Old, I'm Old Get Used To It!* Marcel Proust said, "Let us be grateful to people who make us happy, they are the charming gardeners who make our souls blossom."[7]

NANCYLEE, RANCH BOSS SAGE

Nancylee Kennedy came quietly into my life when I first moved to the Hill Country of Texas in the early nineties. We shared a spiritual path as students of metaphysics for many years. Then she became one of my Tai Chi students, always faithful to our class right up to the time she went in for knee surgery and then looking forward to returning to our class. She was dedicated to learning this dancelike, meditative form of martial arts. Looking back, I see that her courage, devotion, and unwavering commitment to be herself have always been my teacher by example. She described her present home as her lovely little cabin. It was built in her honor. The gratitude she felt for it shone through the sparkle in her eyes and warm smile. Sharing her wisdom, her candid acknowledgment of her struggle within her own journey toward sagedom, is my grand privilege. Nancylee describes herself as the range boss of Quiet Valley Ranch. This property, which she and her then husband Rod Kennedy bought in 1973, became the home for the Kerrville Folk Festival, which they had begun in the early seventies. The Kerrville Folk Festival is the longest continuously running music festival of its kind in North America. For eighteen straight days and nights each May and June, guests come from all over the world to experience the magic of music made here. The festival is known internationally as a Mecca for singer-songwriters of varying musical styles. Those just developing their skills have the opportunity to play their music alongside master craftsmen, sometimes around late-night campfires. One definition of "range boss" is one who provides levelheaded senior guidance. And I think that is what Nancylee did for the folk festival. For many years, she delivered her wise and pithy "bumper sticker" ideas on Sunday mornings at Quiet Valley's Chapel Hill, adding depth and thought to these eighteen days of musical fun. I invite you to experience some of her story in her own words.

I. Leahanna Young

One of my human failings has been wanting for so long to write the script for the lives of people I care about. Surely with just a few adjustments from me, they would be near perfect. This is a seemingly commonplace characteristic among those of us who are people fixers. How hard I've worked to eliminate this trait and how deeply tied into the essence of my being I found it to be. It wasn't until other changes entered my life that I have been able to begin to let it go.

One change is the recognition of the beauty of the me I am inside and the acceptance of the manner in which that wonderful self has finally begun to emerge. It's as though my entire life has been unfolding toward the understanding of my relationship to the whole of creation. How easy it is to accept and love myself in the light of my continuity. With self-acceptance, I can openly love and accept others at whatever step they find themselves in their own journey. How could I deny another joy of working through his or her own maze of self-creativity and truth-seeking? To interfere would be arrogant. After all, I was never given power or authority over any other human being.

What beautiful connection it was to discover that the essential quality of one of my most treasured friendships is total acceptance. I wouldn't change him for the world, although I think he would find greater fulfillment if he made some changes in his life. Also, his relationships with those we both love are his relationships, not mine, and I keep my hands off, one of my hardest releases. It is my role to stand by and endorse his own self-creation and discoveries and to occasionally share in his joy of finding his own truths as he experiences them. All these will unfold in God's time.

With this precious example to go by, I would hope that all my relationships would center on acceptance. How lovely it is to say in your heart, "I love you, my friend, as you are and where you are."

So now . . .

I Claim

I finally claim my freedom to be me, not anyone else and not how anyone else perceives me, but the me self that God created for me alone to live. How much easier it is for me to be me than to try to be anyone else.

I Choose

I choose to be in the company of those who invite me to be who I am, who, without wanting to alter me, encourage the "who I am" to be released. I seek out those who foster my becoming more and more of who I am.

I Am

Stress comes from trying to be someone we are not. It takes no extra energy to be ourselves. I'm not all I want to be, but I'm going to be me during my becoming.

Today our lives are bombarded by constant chatter and assaulted by "verbal vegetation," which leads me to value life's messages that are succinct and very much to the point. These messages are meaningful to me and have been, in many ways, clichés to live by. Among those I have gathered and collected are messages that are known as "bumper stickers." Here are a few of my favorites:

- A true friend is someone who sees you as you want to be . . . even before you're becoming.
- We forgive, not because they need it, but because we need it.
- Projects turn out better when no one cares who gets the credit.
- From what we get, we make a living; from what we give, we make a life.
- What your eyes alone see is seldom the total picture.
- Help wanted? Inquire within.

- When thanked for a favor, just say, "We're all here to reach out to each other."
- Our Earth is on loan from our children.
- Don't spend your life in regret.
- Facts alone don't always lead to truth.
- A man's character is revealed his last day on the job.
- Jesus came not to declare his own divinity, but to show us ours.
- There's no such thing as a free puppy! (my favorite)

I was not present for Nancylee's Sunday morning sessions; however, knowing this sage, I can envision that the spiritual jewels she offered were accompanied by funny stories that helped open minds. To imagine how a Sunday lesson could be crafted out of "There's no such thing as a free puppy" gave my own "playful puppy" mind a chance to run, scamper, and cavort around. It retrieved ideas such as:

- Everything comes with some responsibility to care for, to love, and to protect.
- If I think it has little worth because it seems free, I miss the treasure it holds for me.

Now it's your opportunity to pick a bumper sticker and see what wisdom you can glean from it or create one out of your own wisdom. Have fun.

Illustration #5

Nancylee Rangeboss Sage

Build Balance into Life

Beware of the bareness of a busy life.[1]
Socrates

*An error doesn't become a mistake
until you refuse to correct it.*[2]
O.A. Battista

Remember the fun of playground days? It may be days of your childhood or, for many parents and grandparents, the joy of being a child again on playground equipment. Some playground equipment is designed to teach lessons of balance, such as the balance beam. Playing on the balance beam teaches the lesson of balancing the body, full focus of attention, and awareness of when a slight lean is needed to maintain balance while slow, thoughtful shifts of weight from one foot brought forward while the remaining foot maintains stability. When beginning this lesson, a parent or friend nearby to touch when the shift is happening assists in keeping balance. Gradually, we learn how to negotiate this beam by providing our own support of shifting weight. How like life this early lesson is.

Another balance teacher found on the playground was the seesaw. A balance lesson we learned here was that the weight on each end had to be balanced if the fun up-and-down motion happened smoothly. That meant, if one child was bigger and heavier, that weight needed to be shifted to the middle. Otherwise, no rocking up-and-down motion happened. Imagine how we can apply these early lessons to our daily life. All these are useful tools for making life easier and fun for all.

Jan, my first twelve-step sponsor, gave me a blank journal, pen, and quiet space. In her wisdom, she recognized how in need of balance my life was. My cup was not running over, but nearly dry because of my lack of balance between doing and being. I was a single mom, working at least one full-time job and sometimes adding a part-time job to make ends meet. My life was giving, giving, giving, which, at the time, I thought was being good. I was carefully following my childhood teaching: God first, others second, and self last. I saw no choice. I had no time to even notice the possibility of another choice.

So in 1988, Jan handed me a beautiful pen and a journal. She then gave detailed instructions to start each day by writing a letter to God in a specific sequence:

- Begin with something for which you are thankful.
- Then get real. Write anything you may feel, including guilt, fear, remorse, concerns, or a confession to yourself and the God of your understanding. Trust that, of course, God knows already. You need to free yourself by acknowledging the feelings, being willing to make amends if so led, and releasing what is past in order to be ready for what is yet to come. Doing this frees you to be fully present in this new day.
- Write your commitment to do only what is yours to do this day as the Spirit guides you.
- Put down the pen and sit quietly.

A knower within you will give you guidance for your day. Recognize that thoughts that bring peace are from that divine knower. Thoughts that contain any element of fear or demands such as "have to" or "must" are from that inner critic that resists peace. Feelings or ideas of guilt, our own or others, are attempts to separate us. They come up to be released so we can focus on action that heals.

This practice has become a lifetime habit for me to savor. Each of my children and grandchildren are aware and honor my early morning time for it. Once my seven-year-old granddaughter Sarah came to me saying, "Grandi, my friend wants to write a letter to God in your book."

So we all went back upstairs, and I pulled out my simple black-and-white composition book. Her friend sat quietly writing her letter while Sarah and I honored her sacred time and act.

The practice of starting my day with my letter to the divine has brought much peace into my life. It is a great help to start my day with the intention to mind my own business. It opens me up to each day's joys and lessons. It increases my sense of the value of being present to all life's beauty, amusing happenings, close connections with others, and even life's pain and sadness. Beginning each day this way directs my energy toward doing only that which is mine to accomplish.

Balance is needed in all areas of life. We need to balance work and play, rest and activity, and alone time and people time. No doubt you can take an honest look at your life and notice additional areas that, as you build in balance, will enrich your life experience. To do this, we must first do what twelve-step work calls an honest and fearless inventory of our life. It is recommended that you share that with your own divine guide and a trusted friend. This aids you in being accountable to build in balance needed and eliminate the blocks to doing that.

Enjoy the Mystery of Life's Journey

The most beautiful thing we can experience is the mysterious. It is the source of all true art and all science. He to whom this "emotion" is a stranger, who can no longer pause to wonder, or stand rapt in awe, is as good as dead. His eyes are closed.[1]
Albert Einstein

Mystery is what happens to us when we allow life to evolve rather than having to make it happen all the time.[2]
Pema Chödren

A friend says, "The problem with knowing is thinking you know." How do you suppose thinking we know is a problem? Thinking we know deactivates our curiosity. We cannot be teachable when we think we already know.

Once on a trip abroad, we had a knowledgeable and entertaining tour guide. Day after day, he pointed out interesting sights, giving thorough background information of each one. His skill for transporting our imagination to carry us into the happenings and people who were part of another time enriched our experience of each. A few people on the tour had taken it before and were excited to tell of the knowledge they had. They repeatedly interrupted our guide.

He was exceptionally patient until the end of a long day when he was clearly not feeling well. We entered a museum in Naples. As soon as everyone was inside, he used this unusually masterful technique for reclaiming his assigned role. He said in a voice with a tone of urgency,

Quickly, quickly, *la famiglia* (Italian phrase of honor by which he referred to our group), gather round. I have essential information to give you. [All eyes turned quietly on him.] In this place, we are going to be as little children who have never seen such beautiful sights before. We will look as though for the first time as if looking through the eyes of a child.

It worked, and us first-timers were relieved to have the unfolding mystery revealed through our more capable guide. If you are to enjoy the mystery, you will see all the beauty of life's mystery new with each viewing.

Why does a good mystery intrigue us? It keeps us turning the pages to the next revelation. When I was a child, the movie theaters showed a Saturday afternoon matinee for kids. It often included a cliffhanger. The hero or heroine was on cliff of peril, ready to fall, and we heard, "Come back next week for the next episode of . . ."

Yes, many of us love to read or see a mystery of another's life. Yet the mystery of our own life is troublesome. Many need to know for sure before they take another step in the journey of their life. That need to be sure of the end becomes the end of adventure's joy and the beginning of worry and stress. If this takes us over, we are stuck in the illusion where we can only be safe by staying where we are on the journey. If any unknowns are brought to our attention, we quickly make up an answer.

A great way to enjoy the mystery is to be in happy anticipation of the unknown. The cliffhangers were exciting because we didn't know for sure what was next. Like it or not, our life has many cliffhangers to be faced. How we face them is the key to whether they produce fear or curiosity. Our false self drags us into the fear of the disastrous possibilities. Our true self surrenders into the grand possibilities of surprising better outcomes than we alone can control or imagine. A bit of wisdom that can keep us in the best possible outcome says, "If you have a dream you think you can accomplish alone, then it isn't big enough."

Letting go of the need to manipulate for a perfect outcome can relieve a lot of stress at best. Even when manipulating or exercising extreme control makes the outcome we thought necessary happen, it is often not as satisfying somehow as expected. To just do our part and invite optimistic others to be part of our dream is good insurance against entrapment in fear and for continuing to enjoy the mystery of our best possible life unfolding.

The fiction of the possibility of obtaining a black-and-white answer can lead us to fill in the unknown inaccurately because we are not ready for the further understanding we demand. Notice that, when we have put into practice what we do know and understand, more is often revealed. If you hear someone reply to new information with "Yes, but," he or she may be resisting practicing the known while asking for that for which he or she has not grown into readiness to receive.

Being in the mystery of your own life is different from needing to keep your life secrets hidden away out of fear of rejection. It is about peeling off the many layers of your false self to discover ever more of what is true about your best self. Like peeling an onion, this may produce tears of joy, relief, or regret for having accepted beliefs of others about you. When we accept the beliefs of others without making them our own, we may limit all we can now choose to be.

In *Mysteries of John*, Charles Filmore writes:

> There is a creative force constantly at work in man and all creation, but is not recognized. It is Spirit-mind shining consciously in the minds and hearts of those who recognize it. Those who ignore this light do not "apprehend" it, and to them it is nonexistent.[2]

Charles Filmore had a burning desire to understand the scripture of the Bible, which to him was holy and often misunderstood, because we fail to go beyond its surface story. He spent his lifetime studying the deeper meanings in order to understand its mysteries and thus apprehend the light he found within himself.

There are those who, in their failing to apprehend this Spirit-mind within, unconsciously accept a story of who they are. Instead it can be easier to accept what relatives pass on about their identity and choose not to make any waves of questioning. This unquestioning acceptance may rest on ideas conveyed through comments overheard or attitudes observed as children. At times, it is verbally expressed in the form of, "In our family, we always vote for this party. It is the party that has our best interest in mind, and it is the best."

It may even be a historically based identity through spoken words or practices we are handed such as, "Those people can hurt you. They just don't think and live like we do. You are only safe when you stay close to your family because the world is a dangerous place. You never know for sure who to trust other than your immediate family."

No doubt, you can think of many other mysterious stories that people accept as their identity without question. Without questioning, they find themselves imprisoned in an image of themselves that limits their lives. These traps prevent us from being in the mystery of our own journey. They are prisons that often times include both fear created by a past we have not personally lived and a future that is only a projection of that unlived past.

To step into the mystery of our own journey is a step into the now. This step facilitates our full presence here and now. It allows us to connect without fear and live a life based on our personal experience of this moment. In this step, we sprout our wings to fly into the unknown with confidence. This is the journey that sets us squarely in the mystery of our own life. This is a trip to relish as we see new scenery, meet new people, discover new talents, and peel every false self layer with new strength for the journey.

Yolanda, Sage of Reconciliation

> Yolanda Pickard has valiantly lived the mystery of her own life. You are about to see how faithfully Yolanda peeled the layers of her history, including, at times, a strength to defend her own treasured culture, to become the sage she is today as she reconciled with herself and her God. Born Mexican American, she has a willingness to claim all the gifts of that heritage. Never did she allow prejudices of others to limit her thinking or her life. At the time of this interview in her ninth decade, she was teaching French at the local university. In addition to her own attitude and loyalty to her family heritage, she opened to sages of the past and her own lifetime. Those gave her assurance and comfort when needed and inspired her to grow within and beyond her own culture.

I. Leahanna Young

RECONCILIATION

> Walls are brought down
> by painful stress
> moving the bricks
> that are set
> and stubbornly refuse
> to give.
> Water can soften crusts
> and wash away mortar
> to release
> the blocks.
> Much can be spanned
> and set free
> if one will but gird a cloth
> and bend
> to wash another's feet.
>
> Yolanda Pickard.

St. Teresa of Avila has certainly impacted my life. I love the fact that she was down-to-earth and yet a saint. I love her mysticism. St. John of the Cross has also affected me. I love his poetry and his love of God. President and Mrs. Roosevelt have greatly inspired me because of their concern for the poor. And of course, Martin Luther King Jr. and Mahatma Gandhi taught us that we are all worthy because we are all God's children.

I've seen how becoming intimately acquainted with these sages and their experiences connects us with God and, therefore, hope. Sages face the challenge of being constantly misunderstood. Sages are more evolved and on another plane, broadcasting their messages from a different frequency than most tune into. Therefore, many cannot understand their point of view. Often, we are tempted to judge those whom we do not understand and often condemn, at times even kill.

That acknowledged, thankfully, I do sense that those around me value my experience and what I have learned from life. They may not follow my lead, but I am made to feel that my opinion matters, even if it is not followed. I feel good about this because I don't want to impose my opinions on them. I am speaking of my family who listens to me and then continues to follow their own way. My students seem to appreciate my opinions, but I'm sure they follow their own path.

My grandparents had a big influence on my life. They loved me, cared for me, and gave generously to me. They planted me in Catholicism. My grandparents cared for me and constantly told me that I was smart. My grandmother called me an "old soul." I feel they passed their faith and wisdom on to me.

My mother was there for me through the years in many ways. As I was growing up, she would remind me, "You have no father so you must protect yourself. Mexican men know there are severe consequences if they disrespect a man's daughter."

I took her warning into my young heart and mind. Once at school, when a boy who was blocking my way threatened me (perhaps playfully), I heard a deep, tough voice coming from my mouth as I commanded him, "Step out of my way, gringo."

Mother provided another kind protection of my virginity. She saved her meager income to go into Mexico on my behalf. Her purpose for this trip was to carry my promise "to maintain my virginity to offer to my husband" to Our Lady of San Juan de los Legos. I was a virgin when I married at sixteen and remained so for the first month afterward. Once again, Mother volunteered yet another support when I went to her in tears because I could not consummate that marriage. She took me to a priest in our village, a compassionate and wise man.

Having known me many years, he told my mother, "She does not love this man, or this problem would not exist."

Also, I told mother I feared the physical pain I'd heard was a part of consummating that union. Mother then took me to a doctor. He put me to sleep while he broke the hymen. I now see that my husband also could sense my lack of love for him, and even though the doctor ended my fear of physical pain, it did not end my husband's pattern of seeking love elsewhere. This led to still more pain of divorce and robbed me of permission to take communion in the church in which I had been planted and grown to love dearly.

I. Leahanna Young

By this time, I had two children who kept me quite busy. For a while, I didn't feel lonely. Then one night, I saw a man I'd known for a while headed to celebrate New Year's Eve in party attire. That night, an unexpected sense of loneliness overtook me. After putting my children to bed, I knelt by my bed and told my Heavenly Father of my plight.

I told Him, "I trust you and know You know all about me. I trust You know, too, of a good man who needs me as much as I need him."

Then I got into bed and fell into a trusting slumber. At midnight, the phone rang, and it was Bill, the man I'd seen on his way to the party. He was calling to tell me the people at the party were boring him and he looked forward to seeing me that next day. I knew my prayer had been heard and answered. Soon, we were deeply in love.

One night, he looked in my eyes and said, "Yole, I love you with all my heart, but—"

"But what?" I anxiously asked.

I felt the Holy Spirit step in to help me hear his answer.

"But you are Mexican."

This time, totally out of character of my usual reaction to such a referral to my heritage, that deep, rough voice of defense of my culture became quiet. From somewhere within me, I heard my own calm but strong voice reply, "The man who marries me must be strong and courageous and respect me for who I am inside, not how I may appear outside. If you cannot do that, then you are not that man. Now you go. Think about that, and let me know."

For a while, we stood in the silence of the weight upon us both.

Then turning to go, he looked back with great concern and asked, "Will you still be here?"

"I'm not going anywhere. I'll be right here. Now go."

In about an hour, he called to propose, and my precious Mexican heritage was never an issue between us.

Next, we were faced with the reality of the disapproval of our union all around us because of our differing cultures. Soon, we realized that we must find a new home. His plan was to go into Mexico, where he thought he could find work as an engineer. God seemed to have another plan for us that moved Bill to El Paso, the result of a job offer from RCA as a missile engineer. This allowed us to marry and be together in El Paso. Because his work took him away from home for periods of time, I enrolled in the university, where I completed my bachelor's and master's degrees in Spanish with a minor in French. Then a series of events led Bill to a job with Raytheon and eventually an assignment to France. This let us move as a family to Paris, where I continued my study of French. That job with Raytheon became a lifetime career for my husband. We felt so blessed we often referred to his company as "Momaray."

Years later, the Spirit was at work in my life, ready to solve the pain of disconnection from full participation in the church I loved. Another caring priest, this time in Paris, France, acted to ease that pain for me. He saw the tears I shed at the time of communion, and I confided the story of my first marriage.

"We are going to fix this," he assured me.

Then he completed the annulment process that freed me to once again enjoy the welcome into communion with my Lord.

Now from my ninth decade, I have great concern that there is a lack of honor given to the elders in our country. The contributing factor may be the way we live. Families used to live close by, and the elders were respected. Families would eat together and share their problems and opinions. The elders were able to share their wisdom and support. Perhaps this deepened our respect for them.

I believe the "everything goes" culture separates people because the older generation cannot go along with it. On the other hand, the older generation can learn to be more accepting of new ways, providing they are not degrading and show respect for elders. There should be love and pride in belonging to a family that flows generously between the young and their elders.

I've seen how the sense of family and pride in it gives value to every member, including the elders. Faith and tradition should play a big role as well. Our family tradition of Saturday morning laxative to cleanse the body and afternoon confession to cleanse the heart and mind in preparation for Sunday communion has done much to keep me feeling clean and free through my life.

CRITIQUE THE CRITIC

*The quality of our life depends
on the quality of questions we ask.*
    Rex Stevens Sikes[1]

The meaning of critique used here is to analyze with unbiased discernment. It is essential to the development of a sage to develop a skill for considering information when it is presented in a way that seems critical. This skill rests on our ability to resist taking it personally. To accept or reject opinions or criticism automatically without using a method of analyzing or critiquing can rob us of useful learning and even our peace of mind. If it takes away our peace, it can cause us to shut down our hearts and minds.

Repeatedly, we find ourselves discouraged by criticism. Often, criticism triggers our hidden doubts of our own abilities. Most people have an inner critic that is easily reinforced by criticism from without. This inner critic teaming up with the outer critic serves to sidetrack us.

Making friends with our critics frees us from taking criticism and using it against instead of for ourselves. Henriette Anne Klauser, in *Writing on Both Sides of the* Brain, describes one technique for making friends in our minds with critical messages. She suggests an internal interview with the critic to better acquaint us with what is true. By knowing the motive of the source of criticism, we can sort what is useful from what is destructive.[1]

Picture such an interview in your mind. It can take place with either an inner or outer critic. Ask yourself questions like these:

- Is this message being repeated with unnecessary emphasis?
- What body language accompanies this criticism?

- What does my own experience and intuition tell me about the value of this?
- Does this call me to continue with my journey or abandon it?
- Is there any compassionate understanding of me here?
- Where in this message do I hear respect for me?

This getting acquainted may include learning to use our own voice to acknowledge what is useful. One phrase for helping us disempower harmful criticism is to say, "Thank you for sharing." Silently or verbally saying this is one way to avoid a debate. This gives time to decide if there is anything useful in the criticism and silently dismiss what isn't a fit.

It is often helpful to have a second opinion from a professional we trust to distinguish between the harmful and helpful. However, use caution in making outside voices authorities that replace our inner knowing.

As we gather wisdom along the journey, we will meet both companions who share or admire our passions and those who do not. Some may fear the passion demonstrated effectively if they see the change its truth calls for in them. This fear may trigger in the critic a need to tear down or deliver criticism in a way that distracts from its value. Elders know how to offer their wisdom with compassion. Criticism offered with understanding comes from a desire to connect and encourages the receiver to see his or her own strengths.

When we can disengage the criticism from the critic and ourselves, we can see both more clearly. We can claim what is true or not about the criticism without judging either party. Then we can acknowledge to ourselves if some tender spot in us has been touched. If this is the case, we may need a more objective view from outside the situation. Critics may be giving their opinion out of a need to prove their own superior knowledge or skill. In some cases, the motive may be to fill a need to have their own competency affirmed.

When we just observe this silently without labeling or judging, we can turn potential hurt into compassion for the critic. In this compassionate seeing, we can understand that the criticism tells us more about the critic than what is being criticized. Remember the critic delivers his or her feedback from his or her own personality and opinions, which may or may not be in line with yours.

The practice of compassion for the critic and empathy for self are aids to escape the traps of anger that do not serve us or self-pity that dissolves our passion to continue. Marshall Rosenberg, in *Nonviolent Communication: A Language of Life*, conveys information on giving self-empathy. Rosenberg emphasizes the importance of doing this when our own inner critic goes on a rampage. This effective tool saves time, energy, and even relationships. It is one way to stay focused on our own purpose and passion.[2]

A Buddhist teaching that aids in giving self-empathy is *mitre*. *Mitre* is holding unlimited loving kindness toward oneself. Here we learn the strength in responding to our inner critic with this attitude of limitless, loving kindness. This is not an escape from personal responsibility. Instead, once we have given this loving kindness to the self, we are better prepared to see clearly what does or does not need to be changed. This is a way to avoid the trap of either—or thinking. This either—or perspective leads us to see ourselves as the victim of the criticism in need of defense or the critic as an enemy in need of attack. By acknowledging within how difficult this is to hear, we free ourselves to claim the truth of who we are beyond what is being criticized. We reassure ourselves that we have the resources to change anything we decide to. This practice can facilitate the use of criticism without judging the critic or ourselves. A Buddhist nun who has written and lectured on this principle with humor is Pema Chrödren.

The critic and criticism they deliver can evoke various responses. A personal reaction may depend on who delivers the criticism, the tone and style of delivery, as well as the mind-set of the one who receives it. Pay attention to feelings that appear in you when you hear words such as the ones below:

- "She is a critical person."
- "Her criticism helped me improve."
- "Her criticism was not helpful to me."
- "She must be crazy because the cops came and took her out of here."
- "The police came and escorted her to safety. I hope she is all right."

We can see the forms our inner and outer critics take by the choice of words that reflect judgment or compassion. See how tone of voice, body language, and use of neutral words or words of judgment all reveal much about all critics. These distinctions will alert us to the wise use of critics. Taking in information from such attention given is important to our journey from no one to wise one.

VICKI, LEARNER SAGE

Wisdom is wisdom the source cannot matter[1]
Paula Underwood, recorder of
Iroquois wisdom in *The Walking People*

> Vicki Marsh has used her many opportunities to be a learner effectively. She came into my life through our common interest in two wisdom paths, the Iroquois wisdom and the wisdom of a Jewish psychologist, Marshall Rosenberg. Marshall developed a way for people to communicate called nonviolent communication or radical compassion, as teachers Jim and Jori Manske refer to it. Through our years of studying these two paths, I was surprised when this sage threw me a curveball by revealing her military career. I was fascinated to discover how the many paths of her life were woven together to create this sage woman who shares her life with us here. Like other sages, she describes her experience of this sharing as a humbling one.

I started my journey of this life on a ranch outside Rapid City, South Dakota. At night, we could actually see the lights of Mt. Rushmore from our ranch home. My schooling began in a one-room country schoolhouse. There, I gained my lifelong love of reading that has aided me throughout my life. That, along with the entire individual attention our teacher was able to give her small classes, was the beginning of my lifetime of rich learning opportunities. From there, we moved to a town near St. Louis, Missouri. Here, I learned discipline as a non-Catholic in an all-girls Catholic school. Finally, I entered and graduated from public school in Corpus Christi after another family move. Next, after graduating from a local university with a secondary education teaching certificate, I taught English in a middle school in San Antonio, Texas. While there, I lived in an apartment complex where there were a number of air force nurses. Their stories of adventure brought back to my mind my mother's exciting stories of serving her country during World War II as a marine airplane mechanic. Assessing my situation, I was aware these nurses were making more money than I was as a teacher. Plus, they were traveling, which I couldn't imagine doing on my salary.

    I began to talk to military recruiters and felt my best choice was to enlist with the marines, in part because they courted me. I soon found myself in Officer Candidate School (OCS) in Quantico, Virginia. I had resigned from my teaching position where there were seven candidates for every job. I did not comprehend until I got to OCS that the marines could discharge me for cause. I now realized I had burned my bridges by leaving my teaching position and chose to endure and keep accepting every opportunity offered me to learn and advance. After my commissioning as a second lieutenant and while attending the Basic School at Quantico, which all lieutenants must go through to be able to perform essential duties, I realized, even though the marines were recruiting women, they were not yet prepared to equip us for field duty. Our utility uniform consisted of a short-sleeved, blue cotton shirt, bloomer-type cotton pants, and black lace-up corfam oxford shoes. Unlike leather, corfam does not breathe, which resulted in hot, sweaty feet and blisters. We used rubber bands to blouse our pant legs over our socks to protect our legs. This adaptation did not work well, however, and we returned with chigger-infested legs and minor injuries not sustained by men who were properly outfitted and wore boots for field duty, for example, orienteering.

    When I found out my future duty station was in Havelock, North Carolina, I cried because I could not find it on the map. My initial military occupational specialty started in public affairs for which I received appropriate training. For a brief time, I served as the press officer in charge of putting out the weekly base newspaper. Another shift in plans found me as assistant personnel officer at a large headquarters and headquarters squadron at Marine Corps Air Station Cherry Point, North Carolina, where I felt that I could better serve marines. Then I was selected for transfer to 2nd Marine Aircraft Wing as one of the first women to serve in the operating forces, the Fleet Marine Force. There, I served as the officer in charge of an administrative assistance and inspection comprised of four senior staff noncommissioned officers. This entailed teaching young marines. My staff saw me as being very hard on them because I would not allow them to drink alcohol on their lunch breaks before afternoon classes began. No doubt my experience as a middle school teacher served me well in commanding their respect for the rules I set for them even while they complained.

I served in a variety of command and command positions over twenty-six years. At one point, I traveled ten thousand miles from Quantico to a base in Okinawa, where I met the man who was to become my husband and life mate.

I was selected to go to all three levels of professional military education courses, including the Naval War College. This was an honor extended to only the top six percent, and I received it with gratitude. There, we studied the details of many wars, and I realized how long people have been killing each other, even family members in the civil war, in the name of a cause. It had a profound effect on me, and I could easily understand how combat resulted not only in mass casualties but also how nightmares plague many veterans for the rest of their lives.

I also learned something in my student teaching days that I used throughout my Marine Corps career, now called imagery rehearsal therapy. It was most useful when, as a colonel, I assumed command of one the Corps' largest battalions with over sixteen hundred marines. This is a kind of "acting as if," which is useful when placed in situations for which you feel ill prepared for taking on responsibility. It called to my mind my mother's voice saying, "The only thing you can rely upon is your ability to adjust."

Another voice in my head was that of Eleanor Roosevelt saying, "You must do that thing you think you cannot."[2]

Often, the voices of wise women in my head let me step into positions of leadership. One such woman of wisdom was Brigadier General Gail M. Reals, USMC (Retired), who said, "Keep your own counsel." I read the message, "Don't let them see your vulnerability."

The experience and advice that lingers in my head came also from men, men with heavy responsibility, such as General George Patton, who encouraged his troops with "Don't take counsel of your fears!"[3] Major General Ray L. Smith, USMC (Retired), was an imposing man with steely blue eyes and distinguished gray hair. He seemed cold and intimidating to me at first, but I learned he had a big, warm heart. His sage words ever remind me to "do right and fear no man."

My last assignment was at II Marine Expeditionary Force at Camp Lejeune, North Carolina. In 1997, after following protocol and submitting my resignation request to Headquarters, Marine Corps, I thought it a common courtesy to advise my immediate senior about it. When I told him I was retiring the following year, he said, "Well, I am going to work your tail off."

I took personal offense that he would even suggest I might slack off because I was retiring. Because the Marine Corps is the smallest of the military forces, we are known by our reputation, which often precedes us. In my twenty-sixth year of service, after proving myself once again not only to my supervisor but to my fellow colonels as well, this same man recommended me for one of the highest awards given, which I received upon my retirement. I left the command in far better shape personnel wise than I found it. Nevertheless, I left with a bitter taste in my mouth due to the less than professional treatment over personnel assignments that I received from my peers, some I had served with for many years.

A few years ago, as I walked my two new wisdom paths, nonviolent communication and the many Iroquois learning stories, I came to accept that the above hurtful comment might have had nothing to do with me as much as perhaps with his experience with those before me who had formed a concern in his mind.

While in the military, a sense of safety, security, and order was given by following protocol, by giving, receiving, and following commands. When I eagerly stepped out of that world into civilian life, that was no longer quite the way order was maintained.

Perhaps unconsciously, I was ready to learn new ways to guide my life. Finding the two wisdom paths that seemed so compatible, I became eager to learn how to use these guides. Nonviolent communication taught me to realize that universal needs drive my behavior as well as that of others. Either needs met or unmet motivated behavior. First, I needed to learn how to identify the need behind a behavior and the accompanying feelings that drove my behavior and others. Taking time to consider this before making decisions made choosing what to do next more effective. The use of a phrase taught by Rosenberg, "Would you be willing to . . ."[4] was a happy replacement for requests that, at times, were ignored or created resentments and distance among myself and those with whom I desired to maintain cordial relations.

The Iroquois learning story, "Who Speaks for Wolf," fit perfectly. It helped me see the value of considering even those not physically present that would be affected by my decisions, how such consideration led to conserving much energy down the road.

The four-step path is another tool I've added from Paula's Iroquois tradition called "The Great Hoop of Life." This is a useful way to make decisions. It is a cyclic path. You walk it in a circle, beginning in the north. You stand in the place of the north, willing to be who you are. This, of course, entails knowing well who you are in that decision making moment. An essential part is knowing what your present learning style is. It may require one to gather insight of other trusted elders to help you fully know yourself. From there, you move to the place of the east on the circle, surrendering into being where you are now without pretense, accepting your circumstance while walking past denial. Next, you move to the south, where you look around yourself taking in as much information as you can. Last, you move into the west in your consciousness, where you use all the knowledge gleaned from all the visits to the previous directions, now more fully prepared for wise decision-making by the logical next step, decide and do, performed fluidly as if in one action step.

Marshall Rosenberg, PhD, said, "We are dangerous when we are not conscious of our responsibility for how we behave, think and feel."[5]

> Lifelong learning is a trait common to all the sages I know. Vicki's story demonstrates this trait so powerfully.

Sage or Sourpuss, Your Choice: Using Our Power to Choose

We're our own dragons as well as heroes, and we have to rescue ourselves from ourselves.[1]
Tom Robbins

Things turn out best for the people who make the best out of the way things turn out.[2]
Art Linkletter

Have you noticed that people seem to either become sages or sourpusses as they hang around the planet for many years? Which are you preparing to be? Are you learning from life's challenges, or are they embittering you? Do you tell your life story as its heroine or hero, victim, or eternal student? There's good news! We do get to choose. We also have the amazing ability to change our own stories, not by denying what has been, but by writing a new story starting with new choices made today.

Last winter, as I was waiting in the patient examining room, I heard a man, on his way down the hallway outside my patient room, becoming louder and sounding more upset with each step. He was saying, "You mean I have to do this every day for the rest of my life?"

The doctor responded, "Only twice a week."

The patient raised his voice. "But, doctor, you mean for the rest of my life?"

Again, the doctor's calm reply was, "Yes, only twice a week."

"Really? For the rest of my life?" The patient persistently complained as his footsteps echoed down the hall.

This struck me as somehow so funny that the doctor came in to find me laughing.

He looked at me, puzzled. "What?" he asked.

"That man you were talking with in the hall just now? He's clearly older than I am. I saw him in the waiting room. As I listened to his questions, I wondered how much longer do you imagine he thinks the rest of his life will be, and what did you instruct him to do?" I was still grinning.

"I only told him to put drops in his ears." Now the doctor started laughing at how much resistance was expressed at such a simple, easy task.

Do you suppose that man has prepared himself to be a sage or sourpuss? Entering the years of potential sage time, we find many adjustments needed to maintain our hearing and other senses and bodily functions. Those who learned to adjust easily to change along the way can cope with less resistance to what can seem like daily requirements for change of our life habits.

If your choice is to become a sage rather than a resistant grump of a sourpuss, increasing resources can assist you. I hope you find both inspiration and education for your journey in this book and its life stories of sage people who consciously made that choice over and over again.

In *The Elder Wisdom Circle Guide for a Meaningful Life* by Doug Meckleson and Diane Haithmore, the life experience of many elders have gathered to form a network through which young people can seek advice on topics of life we all face, such as relationships, job decision making, and maintaining a positive attitude.[3] Check out their website at www.ElderWisdomCircle.org.

In this book, Elder Anita, seventy, of Brewster, New York, a retired social worker, shares some insight into how her wisdom was developed. She says, when she was young, the golden rule of teaching, "Treat others as you want to be treated," made sense to her, and it still does. Later as an adult, she faced trying to make sense of the erratic actions of a spouse suffering from mental illness and alcoholism. At that time she picked up another gem of wisdom, "Do not expect rational behavior from irrational people." In her forties, she adopted the wise counsel of Eleanor Roosevelt, who said, "No one can make you feel inferior without your consent."

In her fifties, she discovered, "People always have three choices, no matter what the situation:

- Do nothing and keep complaining; being a victim is your choice.
- Do nothing but stop complaining; learn how to accept your situation.
- Do something different.

If your choice is the second or last, someone can help you. If your choice is the first you don't want help.

Martin "Old Eagle," Native Wisdom Sage

Treat every woman as a lady because you never know what she had to do or where she has been.
Advice Old Eagle's mother gave him

A gentle circumstance brought the three of us together, Martin "Old Eagle" Hays, his "Butterfly Lady" Anita, and me. It was the beginning of a journey he and I are still sharing. Though Anita has taken her final flight, Old Eagle and I continue our weekly meetings at Unity Church of the Hill Country. Early on our journey together, I saw the sage in him, though there was a timelessness about him that kept me unaware of his chronological age. Ten years ago, we celebrated his eightieth birthday. Now I know he was born in 1922. His calm, unassuming nature, his twinkly eyes, and mischievous smile reveal a depth of spirit and wisdom often unspoken. The nature lover and creative artist in both Old Eagle and his lady, Anita, has always been easy for all to see. They both possess that spirit of generosity and appreciation of beauty in all its many forms. After Anita's passing, living without her and with Parkinson's became a challenge he accepted with courage and determination. This journey led him into a wheelchair and then evolved to a walker and then a cane. Today, he walks freely again, living alone with the daily visits of friends to oversee his care. Those who offer this feel enriched by any time spent with him, whether doing his laundry, providing him food, or taking him to church and doctor visits. The Parkinson's has taken away his ability to drive. "I feel a sense of loss of freedom to come and go that wheels gave me," he reports without dwelling on it or allowing it to dampen his spirit. His ability to experience lucid dreaming gives him freedom to travel that does not depend on wheels. "It keeps me always on the move and gives me material for my writing."

His humor aids him in his present life journey and shows up at times during physician visits. Once, the orthopedist asked, "Mr. Hays, what's up with that board across your walker?" Old Eagle said, "Well, doc, if I pick up chicks, they have to have someplace to ride." Once, a female urologist asked him if his urine ever burned. His answer stunned her. "You know, I never tried to light it." There is no doubt as I listen to his story that much of his sense of humor was a gift from his alcoholic father. Old Eagle describes his dad as a happy alcoholic and his mother as a hard-shell Baptist who thought even a drop of alcohol passing through the lips could send one straight to hell. His father was an oil field worker. Martin spent his early years in the flimsy shanties with tin roofs common to all these oil field workers. As is often true of young ones, he was quick to pick up the oil field jargon. Martin adopted the name "Old Eagle" at a point in his life when he began to notice how an eagle was flying over him often when he looked up. He began to see the eagle as his guide. He would talk to the eagle and ask him questions about anything that was puzzling him. Soon, he noticed the answers that came to him when he looked up and asked proved to be right for him. In Native American spirituality, animals are thought to be messengers. The message of the eagle is "Eagle medicine is the power of the Great Spirit, the connection to the divine. It is the ability to live in the realm of spirit and yet remain connected and balanced within the realm of Earth" (Jamie Sams and David Carson, *Medicine Cards*, 41)[1]. Ah yes! Such a fit for this fascinating and inspiring man I've come to know through the years, a bridge that allows me to connect the boy he speaks of with the sage of today. Old Eagle offers the perfect example to those who want to choose sage over sourpuss.

My mother discovered Dad's pattern of coming in the back door when tipsy. She watched him coming home one night and saw him hiding his whiskey under the front porch steps. As Dad headed for the back, she went out the front and retrieved the bottle. She made a show of pouring out the remainder of the whiskey, watching with a look of victory in her eyes as every last drop fell to the ground and looking around in hope the neighbors were watching.

Turning to rush in the front door, meeting her husband in the house as he came in from the back and feeling no pain, she announced with pride, holding up the empty bottle, "I found your whiskey."

Dad's impish comeback was, "Well, it wasn't lost."

One windy night when I was about four years old and the shack was being blown about and making strange noises, I asked my brothers, "What the hell was that?"

"That's the bogeyman who's coming for little boys saying bad words," came my brother's warning.

"Tell him to just come on and I'll kick his ass," I said like I was a giant.

Because of this kind of language, my mother washed out my mouth with lye soap quite often.

At the supper table, Dad would often ask, "Ham, ram, or mutton?"

He knew, as did all us kids, that we had none of the above.

Hoping to entertain as Dad did, I asked Dad's usual question when the minister came for dinner. "Ham, ram or mutton?"

An awkward silence of surprise followed this question. Then mother took me out for the soapy mouth routine to which I was becoming accustomed.

Not only did I play the clown at home, I was also the class clown at school. After many trips to the principal, who administered more and more swats, it became apparent this punishment was not working. Knowing nothing else to try, the teacher would make me sit out in the hall. I spent a lot of time out in that hall. Many times, I watched the principal coming down that hall, holding up a paper he was pretending to read in order to block his vision of me as he walked past.

Even in the midst of all the problems I caused, I was liked, and I managed to learn and more than keep up. I became a candidate for graduation at fifteen years of age. My mother thought I was too young to be out on my own, so she had me held in school another year. I don't remember learning much more than the last year, as it was pretty much a repeat of what I'd learned before. I felt both ready and had great anticipation to be out on my own.

Knowing my father was a Native American and serving in the Marine Corps with many Navajos inspired me to explore the stories of these people. I was fascinated to know more about them and felt somehow drawn to their ways. A story I remember well is of the two wolves.

Inside everyone lives two hungry wolves. There is a good, caring, always helpful wolf whose goal is to win. There is also an uncaring, mean wolf who would never consider helping any one. His goal also is to win. When told this story, children ask, "Well, which wolf will win?" The answer is, "The one you feed." [2]

I learned Native American children were taught through stories, often animal stories in which the animals were given traits and experiences of humans. I knew that the telling of such stories is a technique that master teachers and sages throughout history have used to challenge those with ears to hear.

For a while, I divorced all religious dogma of the world and accepted the spirituality in all beliefs. After some time had passed, I realized what others had told me, "There is only one God. In the many ways that one approaches belief, we should do it with love."

As years passed by, I migrated back to religion to accept it as a teacher, helper, and friend. I found in Unity a church where I could use the truths of Native American spiritual teachings and the love I'd found for Jesus.

Once, I was in a canyon photographing wildflowers. I was especially looking for a flower called the "Ghost Flower" because it grows under rocks and in the most unlikely places. I began to feel so close to Great Spirit that I said aloud, "I love you." That day, alone in that canyon, I knew I was in God's cathedral. At this moment of truth, I fell in love with God.

I cried and told the Great Spirit that I loved Him.

The voice inside me said, "Each one of us is His child. Be proud, and be thankful."

Looking toward the west late that afternoon, the sunset spoke to me very plainly. God was telling me, "I have given you the universe. Go and enjoy it."

People and Things in My Life

Mother: Who showed me beauty in God
Father: Who wrote with his heart
Sister: Who placed loving hands on my wound
Brother: Who laughed a while and then went away
Children: Who taught me not to judge
Grandchildren: Who made me aware of my inner self
Man: Who sits and talks to me of rushing waters and paths made of stone
Woman: A lady who transforms white canvas to beautiful flowers. Who lies down with me and makes the two of us one
Friend: Who gave me friendship? Who said it's okay to cry
People of Despair: Who causes me to stumble and trip over my own ego
People of Humility: Who made me look up to find the underside of a rainbow
Flowers: Who lies down during a rainstorm and then smiles again with the sun
Wind: Who without eyes or fingers finds me on a hillside

I. Leahanna Young

Jesus: Who gave me love? Who made me see and feel love and the miracle cure for a lifetime of loneliness
God: Who gave me the universe
"Old Eagle" Martin (Buster) Reagan Hayes

Martin (Old Eagle) Hays, Artist and Author.
Print from Spirit Paintings Two.

SEGUE INTO A SAGE:
AVOID THE SLIP INTO SENILITY

*Life isn't about waiting for the storm to pass. It's about
learning to dance in the rain.*[1]
Vivian Green

"Segue" implies passing from one experience to another smoothly. Think of segueing into being a sage as adding a new dance step to your repertoire. If you have never danced, learning in the eighth decade may mean lots catching up to do. You may find yourself going back to the tasks of previous decades and completing steps that those who have been moving with the rhythm of life's learnings have mastered.

Those previous dances, whether in the rain or the soft hues of an inspiring sunset, are varied. They are the challenges each decade of our life offers to grow us toward the next. Strangely, for me, one dance has been divorce. Fully experiencing all the feelings of despair, relief, and grief and allowing them to be my teachers has benefitted me. Being fully present to and honoring of that experience opened me to compassion, forgiveness, and patience. All these and others are openings required of a sage. Certainly, divorce is not a dance that is essential or recommended, but it can be an unexpected gift if claimed as such. For some, the opening has been weathering other losses, such as job, health, family, and friends. The dance also includes flying from the nest of childhood home's safety and establishing your own. Answering the questions of "Who am I?" and then "So who am I now?" over and over again is essential to the process. No doubt, as you look back, you can see your own times of change that produced growth because you were honest with yourself through any resistance and acceptance you experienced.

Three of my four grandchildren are now in their twenties. I am a privileged front seat observer to some of their experiences in this developmental stage. In our twenties, the tasks include becoming responsible for our own lives. Often this includes times of breaking away from our parents and birth family in order to do this. Sometimes, this breaking away is painful for both, at times more so for parents. It is a time to try out many roles and explore many possibilities. Tasting different parts of our world and what it offers us expands choices.

Hopefully, families support this with both encouragement and, when appropriate, the sharing of their own experiences. This is done most effectively by recognizing teachable moments of readiness to hear. If willing, people in their twenties will learn from each role tried and the disappointments that inevitably accompany some.

I could have saved myself, and perhaps at least my first son, some pain if I had a firmer grasp of the tasks of this decade. Perhaps the parent may be ready to let go, but the child feels some need to hang on. It can also be a time when parents hang on and the child feels the need to cut the apron strings. This may even result in a period of misunderstanding and alienation for a while. One of the worst mistakes I see parents making is robbing a child of experiencing the consequences of his or her own decisions and behaviors. These consequences experienced may serve as an adult child's most powerful teacher. Of course, there may be life-threatening situations where parental assistance is needed. The teaching power of experiencing the consequence of our own behavior or choice is great. Understanding this power can help parents make wise decisions about when to help and when to let consequence teach its lessons.

As we complete these tasks, we become more independent and responsible for ourselves. As we do so, we acknowledge that the magic age of twenty-one does not a grown-up make. Indeed, there is much growing yet to be done.

When discussing this chapter of the journey to becoming wise with my middle grandson and his girlfriend, he asked me, "Grandi, what tasks am I supposed to be completing during my twenties?"

I commended him on the responsibility I saw him taking for completing his education, as that is an important task of this time of life. I shared that the tasks of taking on more responsibilities were still ahead. When I remarked that twenty-one is not the magic time we had expected, he looked at his girlfriend. They grinned a knowing look of agreement.

Then turning back to me, he commented, "Boy, are we ever learning that!"

Entering the thirties with some exploration behind us, we are more prepared to settle down to establish our more grown-up self. Having built a little wisdom, we may now willingly grow in patience for the challenging task of a more settled life. This often includes developing a career, marriage, home, and, eventually, family of our own. Often, this is the time to begin reconnecting with the family of our roots. As we mature, we can relate more as adult to adult, no longer as dependent child to parent. What a surprise it is to discover we may need to get reacquainted with what could seem like a new parent. This parent who found giving his or her child wings has freed her or him to grow wings as well. The adult child may even delight in this interesting person who now feels more like a wise friend, one that relates to son or daughter as an adult rather than a child needing parenting.

With still more wisdom acquired, we are prepared for our forties. Here, we begin to reap the harvest of the patient, sometimes difficult, not always fun, work behind us. This is the opening for building upon the foundation we've set down. While we are enjoying what past preparation has brought, we come to the diligent work of acquiring things, accolades, and respect. We can even begin to recognize the budding self of the thirties beginning to further bloom. As I entered my forty-ninth year, I was told, in Jewish tradition, this is the year of supreme forgiveness. This seven times seven year allows us to take stock of that which we have postponed forgiving at each seventh year's end. Forgiving is the tool we use to stop the replaying of a one-time event over and over in our mind. The event and the meaning we chose to give it may have produced an initial injury that we compound. We unintentionally wound ourselves by repeatedly rehashing it, often distorting the occurrence and causing us even more discomfort.

It seems it was about here in my life that a wise sage introduced me to a valuable question, "Would you rather be right or happy and at peace?"

When I ask myself that, I become aware of how attached I can become to being right. In that attachment, I then begin to recruit people and evidence to validate my right view and my right to hold it. Resentments, fear, and even hate are such lonely feelings. We unconsciously make them a team sport. However, here is an opportunity to consider our own part in resentments held. That accomplished, we become empowered to truly, not in word only, let go of any past burden, resentment, or hurt, real or imagined. Doing this personal self-inventory, making any amends to others or even ourselves, frees us to fully claim the gift of moving on into our fifties.

William Arthur Ward said, "Forgiveness is a funny thing. It warms the heart and cools the sting."[2]

Now those maturing toward becoming sages begin to consider the "been there, done that, and what now" questions. They consider ways to fertilize that blooming self of the forties who paved the way for the high point of presently viewed accomplishments. This is a chance to give new meaning to what the less mature may have labeled as failures. NASA calls these instances "negative successes."

Here in our fifties, we find a juncture for some reflection and expressions of gratitude. We can begin to release that inward push for more and more of whatever. Our fifties can offer us a point to finally savor what is now part of our present life. For many, this includes a period of spiritual questioning. They may find a readiness and need for a season of going within for deeper meanings of life beyond acquiring. What a good moment for acknowledging the value of what has been and considering some new possibilities ahead.

Ah, now the sixties. Ram Dass speaks of his own experience of this transition point. In a lecture on conscious aging, he reflects on how confusing this time can be for Westerners. When am I considered a senior? Is it when I become eligible for the AARP in my fifties? Must I wait for my Medicare and Social Security to kick in? Having lived a part of his life and done studies in the Eastern cultures he observes, "From zero to twenty, you are a student. From twenty to forty, a householder. Forty to sixty, you are expected to do spiritual studies. Then at sixty, you become free."

Entering the sixties presents a chance to contemplate that which has been finished and to explore something intriguing about to begin. The empty nest has been survived. Some dreams that have previously been told "not now" are still awaiting fulfillment. Our need to contribute may now be filled by mentoring others coming through their life challenges. At last, we may experience the joys of grandchildren, ours to take delight in, who are mainly the responsibility of our own children, their parents. There is a new sense of freedom in entering back into that playful time of life, led by these children, who by no accident are called grandchildren.

This can be a golden age of entering more deeply into relationships with family, friends, and passions that perhaps we had put on hold. Now we can unite without losing our true selves, a surrender without submitting.

A faint voice may call us to see this as a time of retirement, a chance to move on with new tires, new lifestyles, ideas, and roles. Any of these can carry us to exciting experiences. We can now choose to re-create our own self-image. We get to use these new tires or perspectives to carry us into the growing wisdom of maturity. Some, who have until now focused on gaining and acquiring for self and family, feel a desire to know the joy of service to others. Suddenly traveling, giving generously, and receiving graciously may be things of our heart's desire.

Perhaps best of all, we can leave the rat race and savor more simple gifts, as we move more slowly, enjoying the scenery. At last, the portal to serenity has opened for us to walk through when willing and ready.

I. Leahanna Young

In the seventies, here with the tasks of many decades completed, it seems we are offered the right to the title of sage. This is more than a title to hold and to keep in reverence. It is possible to enjoy it with a mostly silent pleasure and a confidence in being who we are without explanation. Our years of completed developmental tasks have taught us the difference between sage and know-it-all. Sages are able to be wise listeners, offering only what is asked, to those who show signs of readiness to receive. Sages notice that, underneath the outward seeming sureness of the know-it-all, there are hints of doubt. This underlying uncertainty is why there may be a need to argue or debate differences, whereas sages are more likely to find some differences both intriguing and inspiring and want to find common ground. In the richness of this common ground, there may come a deepening respect on both sides and a desire to move beyond the need for agreement. With that respect comes an amazing experience called dialogue. This dialogue can even open doors to a more intimate connection of acceptance of differing points of view. The seventies, however, are no longer necessarily the end that those of past generations felt was imminent. There may be more awaiting the seasoned sage in coming generations.

We are blessed to live in an age that lets us look ahead to our eighties, where we see those who are demonstrating the greatest degree of freedom from life's shoulds and oughts. Those sages' eyes twinkle as though they know secrets that are making them laugh on the inside, even when they have the wisdom to recognize those not yet mature enough to enjoy such concealed pleasures.

We may even welcome, rather than dread, our majestic nineties. This is often the result of giving up the fight against a changing body, perhaps through an acceptance of needed changes in our own behaviors. This is where the lion-hearted, the regal thoroughbreds, reside. You may find them still living alone, with family, or in group homes. You will recognize those whose developmental tasks are completed by their contentment with themselves, life, and those they love.

Then on to a great celebration of those called centenarians! So now you may rightly ask, "How does one slip into senility? I thought that was a disease over which you have no control?"

In *Younger Next Year*, Henry S. Lodge, MD, an internist, speaks of his long-term relationship with patients who led him to see that some of his patients were experiencing premature aging or even premature death. This inspired him to do some research. He concludes premature aging and death was not due to poor medical care as much as to inadequate health care. Many of the problems considered to be related to normal aging he found were lifestyle related. One of his patients joined him in co-authoring the book to educate as they entertain people on ways to not only delay but actually prevent many conditions previously assumed to be normal aging.[5]

The dictionary defines "senile dementia" as a syndrome of progressive, irreversible impairment of cognitive function, caused by organic factors and having its onset late in life. How is it then that some reach that late-in-life age of even one hundred with mental facilities still sharp? This is a question to which medical science continues to offer new possibilities. As we live longer, we present more candidates for this study, another gift given by our sages.

You can find several websites that give definitions of senile such http//education.yahoo.com.reference/dictionary/entry/senile[6] Many mention that "senile" comes from a Latin root meaning "old age". Fortunately we have become more sophisticated in our understanding of, what is now termed, "senile dementia." We understand there are several possible causes, some environmental, some functional, and even nutritional. We continue to fine-tune our understanding from a medical, social, and health viewpoint. So do stay tuned. It seems much can be addressed to reduce the experience of many forms of this condition, which was previously thought a natural part of the aging process.

Gary Small, MD, director of the UCLA Longevity Center, has written a book based on his years of experience and research. In the Alzheimer's Prevention Program, he outlines a program for maintaining healthy brain function. Dr. Small says the jury is still out on just how effective as prevention these lifestyles changes can be and further research is needed. He also reports a recent National Institutes of Health consensus did say that many studies of healthy lifestyle habits—including diet, physical activity, and cognitive engagement—are providing new insights into the prevention of cognitive decline and Alzheimer's disease.[7]

What is known and we hear from friends who change to healthier lifestyles is they reported feeling stronger and more vibrant and they have a sense of a more pleasurable life experience. We can also observe some characteristics that are held in common by these rare ones who live longer, healthier lives and remain more mentally astute.

They have stayed active, physically and mentally. The music of the growth dance of mind and spirit has continued in them, even in the midst of bodily limitations. They somehow manage to overcome, detour around, or resist allowing such physical changes to become the focus of life, perhaps by keeping that vital curiosity alive and well in the midst of body mysteries.

An article in *Newsmax Health*, "Hong Kong's Secrets to Longevity," reports Hong Kong's longest life expectancy of 86.5 years. It identifies four activities these Chinese people have as part of their lifestyle.

1. They eat a diet of steamed vegetables and fish along with fruits.
2. They engage in physical exercise. Tai Chi practice improves balance and calms mental activity.
3. Mah-jongg is a popular game for stimulating the brain. Even wedding receptions traditionally include mah-jongg tables. Because it is a game requiring four players and social interaction, it provides for the need to stay socially connected, which can help delay dementia, according to aging expert Alfred Chan of Hong Kong's Lingnan University. To read more, see Hong Kong's Secrets to Longevity.[8]
4. To stay engaged in work with a purpose fulfills a need to feel useful.

Are you Living Yet?

Life is a dance.
Are you living yet?
Do you hear your music?
Are fears of attack, conflict,
Complaints, whispers of doubt
Dulling the sound?
Is some judgment
Drowning your music's call
To begin living?
Listen closely.
Feel life's rhythm beating within you
Hear the hum of your heart
It's your song beckoning
Dance my message of passion-filled life
Come dance, my sacred song
Unite all earth's creation
In celebration of
Dancing sages
Offering wisdom to all

SAGES IN DISGUISE

You have to have darkness for the dawn to come.
Harrison Ford[1]

A sage in disguise is easy to overlook. If we think a sage is a famous person, someone living high on mountaintops, or not likely to be found around us, it is time to open our eyes to other possibilities. We can find sages by looking closer to us as we learn how to see them. Usually there are physical characteristics such as age, countenance that reflects contentment, or a presence that draws people to spend time with them. In that presence, we may find a kind of permission to slow down, to breathe deeper, and to look around and within. An encounter with a sage creates a renewed sense of hope.

Sages are not without their own life challenges. Characteristics common to sages may be blurred by a life situation that requires eyes to see beyond outward appearance. Those eyes grow with our understanding of the sage. It is something like deciding you really want a red car. Suddenly you see red cars where you never noticed them before. Who would think you would encounter a conversation with a sage facing such a life situation when doing your grocery shopping. Still, this is a true story.

I noticed her immediately, standing there in her fluorescent orange sweatshirt. Her face was leathery and wrinkled. She was looking longingly at a small bag of frozen turnip greens. At first glance I thought, "Now there is the beauty of a sage in that weathered face." Then on second look, I saw despair and hopelessness in both her face and posture. Seeing the potential, somehow shaded by something unknown to me, aroused my compassion and curiosity. It was a look one might see from someone poised to jump from a building or bridge. How could that expression be on the face of this woman? As I wheeled my grocery cart toward her, my attention was completely captured. I approached her, and our eyes met.

She said, "You know, I love greens. I'm on Coumadin though, so I'm not supposed to have greens. I can't have cranberries either. The nurse looked at my blood sample report and she said, 'You've been eating cranberries, haven't you?' I had to admit I had. She had the proof. I told my doctor, 'You know, it really isn't worth living anymore. I can't eat so many of my favorite things.'"

I wanted to offer her some hope. "What can you still eat that you enjoy?"

"Oh, sweet potatoes. I love sweet potatoes."

"I'll bet you can have carrots then. Do you like carrots?"

"Oh, yes," she replied. "And cauliflower, too. I love that. I have some at home. The florets, you know?"

She looked thoughtfully at the bag of turnip greens. We stood a moment in silence as I watched her considering. She quietly began measuring the bag of turnip greens into thirds with her hands.

"You know, I bet I could have just a little of these with the cauliflower and sweet potatoes. Then I'll check my blood before I eat them again."

A smile began to take shape. A new twinkle lit her eyes. The desperation fell away from her face. As she looked up at me, again I could envision the sage that, even in times of seeming loss and despair, reaches down deep inside and finds hope and reason to live.

"Sounds like a feast you've planned for yourself!" I was almost able to taste her newfound joy myself.

Two strangers, we stood in the intimacy of that moment and then moved on in opposite directions, nameless to each other but aware of this sacred time shared. I knew I had just observed a sage practicing letting go of what was no longer part of her life.

That willingness to turn loose our hold is part of the preparation that will one day allow for a peaceful, final letting go. I sometimes observed that easy passage when I worked for hospice. That gift is given to those loved ones who then describe the ending of this life experience as a blessing. It is a blessing given by one who was enabled by previous practices for gracefully leaving at the end of this physical life.

Lolyn Alana Young, a sage in the making, said, "In the circle of life there is no finish line."

I listen in wonder as the sages in my life tell the stories of the sages who offered wisdom to them along their way to sagedom. I see how such wise ones appear so unexpectedly in surprising forms and modes of transportation to play their unique role in a life. It is clear how critical each role is in the formation of the sage to whom they appear.

Here is one such fortuitous appearance. This sage rides into the life of a boy in need. Thanks to this wisdom shown a child, the child has become a man who now is a sage in the lives of many.

In the Biblical New Testament Hebrews 13:2 admonishes us, "Do not forget to entertain strangers, by so doing some people have entertained angels without knowing it" May Smokey, this sage on a motorcycle, remind you of that.

Smokey, Sage on a Motorcycle

*Knowledge is a process of piling up facts;
wisdom lies in their simplification.*[1]
Martin Fischer

I never knew my father. The first father figure I came to love entered my life when I was nine years old. The only name I knew him by was Smokey. He was the counselor and case worker I was assigned while I was living at the Washington State Children's Home in Spokane, Washington. I remember the day he came to the home. I was in the dormitory looking through a window down onto the parking lot when Smokey came riding in on a big, red and silver Indian motorcycle. It was the most beautiful thing I had ever seen. Its engine sounded like the soft, yet powerful, rumble of thunder in the distance.

I ran down the steps into the parking lot and just stood there panting like a little puppy. I thought to myself, "When I grow up, I want to be just like him." (I still want to be like Smokey when I grow up!) Smokey could see that I was mesmerized.

He said, "Would you like to sit on my bike? Maybe after I check in, we'll go for a spin."

Oh, I tell you, I felt like a real somebody!

As time passed, my love for Smokey grew deeper and deeper. I remember so vividly the gifts Smokey gave me as we went on what he called "sharing walks." He would go through a ritual that included filling the large pockets of his coat with the things he would use to teach me. One of the gifts Smokey gave me was a fifty-cent piece. At first, my child's mind thought of all the things I could buy with it.

Smokey said, "No, I want you to keep this in your pocket. This coin has a special message for you. I want you to look at it carefully and tell me what it says."

I read the four words, "In God We Trust."

There on that path in the woods with Smokey, I came to know a loving God. My new friend put his hand on my head and said, "Eddy, you don't ever need to be afraid because God's presence is with you always."

On another walk, Smokey reached into his pocket, pulled out a big, red rubber band, and gave it to me.

I thought, "What a dumb thing to give someone."

Then Smokey said, "Eddy, you are like that rubber band. Not every boy in this home will make it in life, but you will. Inside you is all the potential to be anything you could ever dream of becoming. All you have to do is be willing to trust God and stretch that elastic mind of yours so that all of the good that is ready to come to you will come and find room to be in you."

In so many ways, Smokey taught me about the presence of a loving God. He opened the pockets of his coat to the wondering mind and heart of a young boy. The riches he gave me were not to be spent on material things. They went far beyond that. They continue to be mine to spend on life.

I have now lived seventy-five years into this life, and I still wonder if Smokey were Jesus Christ in disguise. "Thank you, Smoky, it wasn't always easy but I'm glad I did."

William Jennings Bryan said, "Destiny is not a matter of chance; it is a matter of choice. It is not a thing to be waited for, it is a thing to be achieved."[2]

> Eddy is now Reverend Eddy and has used his life to show that loving God to others. He and Patty have raised five children. Today Rev. Eddy shows that same love and faithfulness to his wife Reverend Patty of thirty-five years.

Connect with Change:
The Twain Can Meet

*Each of us is great insofar as we perceive
and act on the infinite possibilities which lie
undiscovered and unrecognized within us.*[1]
James Harvey Robinson

*To achieve the impossible, it is exactly the
unthinkable that must be thought.*[2]
Tom Robbins

The phrase "and never the twain shall meet" can be true for those not yet a sage and trying to stay relevant in our culture of youth. I found an effective way to deny that phrase its power. It happened with someone probably in his late twenties, maybe early thirties.

While shopping for a laptop in Walmart, I was fortunate for a young man named John to assist me. I was pleasantly surprised to find how interested he seemed in my need for a laptop. He demonstrated knowledge of the many brands, along with the pros and cons of each. In addition, he shared his own experience with the different options. He told me of the one he preferred when he purchased one for his wife. As he spoke of this, he revealed his need to support his wife in her goals. So when her first choice for a career did not work for her, he encouraged her to choose again. I began to form a sense of an exceptionally devoted husband in this young man, which I admired. At last, after also seeking advice by cell phone from a friend, while John assisted another customer nearby, I made my choice. By this time I was unconsciously feeling like this stranger, John, was my new best friend as he waited patiently, seeming to sense this was a big decision for me.

Finally, I chose one and said to John, "Now I need a carrying case for it."

He was right there to show me the cases available. As I was looking, he casually mentioned his main use of his computer was to play a game called something like "War and Weapons." He said many of his friends enjoyed this game as well.

I took a deep breath as a cloud of confusion engulfed me. I turned to him and said, "John, I am really passionate about peace. Picturing you sitting in your living room at war without even combat pay does not fit the image I had formed of you. Can you help me understand? What fascinates you and your friends about this game?"

"Well," he replied, "it is the weaponry of old that was so artistic and had a kind of beauty."

Slowly, I took this in, and the cloud lifted as I felt our connection again. Art and beauty, I could relate to that. "So have you seen the movie *The Mexican*?" I asked.

"No, I haven't," he answered with an expression that seemed to say I had jumped ahead of him or got left behind after his reference to the video games.

So I explained, "*The Mexican* is not a person, but a beautifully crafted ancient weapon of great value."

His expression changed from puzzlement to heightened interest as he replied, "That sounds like one to put in my queue on Netflix."

This led to an exploration of some possible psychological explanations for his attraction to weapons and war games. "Could it be, I asked him, a particular part of the old male hunter brain or safe release of testosterone? Maybe a way to get an adrenalin rush within the safety of one's living room?"

John, one by one, eliminated any psychological motivation saying, "According to psychological standards, I should be a psycho, given my past."

Now the therapist in me caused my interest to heighten. "So you've been through some trauma?"

"Yeah, my mother took me to a psychiatrist once who told her, 'What can I say? Your husband hates your son, and your son hates his dad.' My dad thought it was a waste of money, so that one session was it."

"Have you resolved this for yourself?" By now, I was feeling a desire for this helpful young man to know peace. He could have been my son, who I would want others to see the goodness in as I had experienced in John during this brief encounter.

"Well, sort of. I did feel curious about how to just use my strengths and let the rest go. So I took a test to identify my strengths. I scored highest in adaptability."

I paid for my laptop, feeling my respect for this young man intact. I sensed that respect had been mutual. Later I reflected on what might have allowed me to remain curious and ask questions that generated responses that maintained a connection. I concluded it was based on the respect I had formed for him that I wanted somehow at some level to protect. The fact that my mind did not jump to label him as one of those young people constantly playing videos games probably helped. I am glad my mind didn't go there. I realized what I would have missed had that had been my instant judgment of him.

I had wished for my sons or grandsons who all live far from me to be with me to guide me through this purchase, but instead, I viewed this stranger as becoming my new best friend. It also raised my awareness of how connected we can all be when we stay open and curious about each other. He could also have labeled me a nosy old lady. His openness revealed he clearly had not done so.

Perhaps therein rests one of the secrets to bridging the gap between generations, one that allows both to profit from connecting with each other. The wisdom and experience of a lady in her eighth decade generation connected with the knowledge and ease of a young man in a generation of constantly speeding up changes and new technology. Many of us find this rapid change to newer technological possibilities challenging at best. Some even find it frustrating to the point of wishing for the return to a simpler time. Could it be that expressing such a wish to go backward to the young may tempt them to label us as old. Instead we can express willingness to share in this time and be here now acknowledging they have help we can use.

Illustration #6

Elder Jack receives cell phone instruction from young
Jason as they span the generation gap

NANCY, THE TEACHING SAGE

When you go out into the world, watch for traffic, hold hands & stick together.
Robert Fulghum

Nancy Gee taught her students all they need to know in her kindergarten classroom. She taught them to live together in compassion and harmony, to learn from everything, and, most of all, to love and respect themselves and others. She came into my life before she entered the years of official sagedom. I was in and out of her kindergarten classroom often because I worked with her students as their school counselor. Looking back now, I know I saw in her even then all the makings of a sage, the kindness, dedication, humbleness of spirit, and, without doubt, a born teacher. Just knowing her with her open, honest heart and always eager to learn more herself let me see that she was a practicing sage before her age moved her into her sage years. Her eagerness to learn was clearly contagious to the children she taught. Never was any child any more or any less than any other in her classroom. One picture is highlighted in my memory. It is the song she sang as she held the hand of a child so proud of new shoes. Together, they skipped around inside the circle of her students sitting on the floor. (There were no desks in her classroom, just a big circle of love and caring.) As she and Jimmy skipped around, she sang, "New shoes, new shoes, Jimmy has new shoes. Hear their squawk. Hear them talk. New shoes, new shoes, Jimmy has new shoes." Everyone celebrated Jimmy's new shoes. Their joy for him was palatable, even among those still wanting new shoes for themselves. Even now, in my own sage years when I am going to bed on clean sheets (a favorite thing of mine), I sometimes sing quietly to myself in the spirit of those kindergartners, "Clean sheets, clean sheets, Leahanna has clean sheets." That night, I always go to bed with a smile. I observed that, not only did Nancy's students love her, in her class, they learned to respect themselves and each other. They became eager learners of everything going on both in and outside the classroom. If something exciting were going on outside that was distracting them from her planned lesson, she would stop and gather the whole class to the window to watch, answering their why questions or leading them to discover the answer. Nancy loved to travel, and she was often one of four women who took a spring break trip together. I was one of the four. It was not uncommon for her to have her own agenda. Nancy's husband Bob was an accomplished attorney and statesman, well known in his community, state and church for his wisdom and generous spirit. He and Nancy were a good team. Walking with the support of leg braces and a cane from serious childhood polio, he still piloted a private plane. He loved showing me how to read an air map and identify landmarks below. I suppose Nancy's ease of exploring on her own may have come about because of his physical limitations. He was determined to live beyond outward appearances. Somehow they had found a way to meet both their needs as they traveled together. When I was once at the end of a relationship that had introduced me to opera, Bob and Nancy found a way to include me in their couple group that explored upcoming operas over dinner as Bob reviewed them for us. Then when I had a surgery that kept me from attending, he made me a taped copy so I could remain connected. This devoted couple raised four children who are now much admired as adults. The many challenges they faced together clearly contributed to their mutual strength and wisdom.

When Bob was alive, he was the one people sought out for advice and to serve on boards and committees. Since Bob died, I am more confident in the wisdom years. Now I am the one asked to serve and get the feedback that I am a great asset. That makes me more secure within myself in these years. Sometimes, someone asks my advice, which I give only when asked. A young family in the church will ask how I handled certain challenges of being a mother of young children. Or because I taught kindergarten, I will be asked child development questions.

I consider how we might create a culture where decision making utilizes the wisdom and experience of its elders along with the vitality and new discoveries of the young. One possibility I think could assist us in combining the two would be:

> Committees and boards at all levels of government could consciously choose a variety of ages and experience. As one who was a teacher of kindergarten for many years, now I am asked to serve on the Miami Public Schools Enrichment Foundation Board. I am asked to chair an important committee at my church, or I am asked if I think a certain candidate for mayor could work well with the town council. I am grateful people now see me as a person of worth beyond the realm of young children. As older people, we need to truly listen to the young to discern what they are thinking and saying. We cannot force our opinions gained from experience, but we can be available to answer questions without being judgmental.

Life is very good for me. I don't feel pressure to try to appear any way but my natural self. The responsibilities of motherhood are past. I am free to choose how I spend my time without the constraints of having to be a certain place at certain hours according to outside expectations.

I. Leahanna Young

> It seemed to me that Nancy always had that freedom to be herself without pretense. In younger years, she took a daily walk with a black trash bag picking up after others, helping keep her neighborhood clean. One day, a big, black car drove up slowly beside her. The driver rolled the window down and handed her an empty soda can. She simply thanked him and continued on her walk, experiencing only amusement that she had been seen as a bag lady. Yet another mark of a sage in the making, knowing who one is without needing to correct any misconceptions others might hold.

Reverend Herman Ging said, "I asked a one hundred-year-old parishioner, 'What has been the best experience of your life?' His answer was, 'The last one.'"

Wisdom of Full Presence

*The attention we pay to the nature of our thinking . . .
is the most powerful attention we can pay.*
Marianne Williamson, *Everyday Grace*

Perhaps you have been the fortunate recipient of the full presence of someone. You knew that there was nothing more important to him at that moment than being with you in the most honest and real way possible. This experience can be magical in its ability to dissolve all thoughts of time and space. For those ready to receive it, a kind of bond can form that we call love. This may be misunderstood as romantic love for it has a taste of euphoria to it. Possibly this can grow into an experience of romantic love at first. Without wisdom to transform that romantic love into a deeper experience of growing together in support of each becoming all they were created to be, it likely will not last.

Whether it goes through a romantic phase or not, it is a great gift. If it continues to grow into a deep and lasting friendship, it will present many opportunities for spiritual growth.

Various spiritual teachers describe this experience of full presence with different terms. One of my teachers refers to it as deep listening. Another says it's the power of being in the now moment. Perhaps you have heard other references, but by whatever description it may be given the gift it brings is healing and a deeper connection with self and often another.

Most sages use meditation or contemplation. Both techniques call us into a deeper space within. It is a time to be fully present to yourself by quieting the endless chatter of your mind. There are many forms of this process.

The most recent form I have practiced is Zen meditation. There I am encouraged to suppress nothing, only to notice everything my mind is thinking. As I label each thought as thinking, I make myself aware that this truly is just a thought and I can choose to let it go. I notice how resistant I am to just being in the silence of peace. This practice allowed me to identify what I label my puppy mind that so loves to play with ideas it can distract me from an important focus.

In Pema Chödron's book, *The Wisdom of No Escape and the Path of Loving Kindness*, she describes meditation:

> Meditation is a process of lightening up trusting the basic goodness of what we have and who we are, and of realizing that any wisdom that exists, exists in what we already have. Our wisdom is all mixed up with what we call our neurosis. Our brilliance, our juiciness, our spiciness, is all missed up with our craziness and our confusion, and therefore it doesn't do any good to try to get rid of our so-called negative aspects, because in that process we also get rid of our wonderfulness.[3]

Further study has shed light on Pema's thoughts for me. Those who have understanding of what psychologists know as a shadow self can use this to make sense of the above. That shadow self acknowledged and managed shows us a path to authentic wholeness. It is not uncommon for this shadow self to appear when we still the chatter of our mind.

Many practices of everyday activities can provide a meditative experience when we are present with our full attention. One I discovered was knitting. I found this unexpected benefit when I was healing from a clinical depression. A neighbor taught me to knit, and I found its calming, healing effects.

For a while, I took my knitting on every trip. It was available when I began to feel a tension-producing rush going on around me. I could always count on my knitting to ground me in peace.

Ram Dass tells a story of his early days of discovering meditation to be a more lasting peace-bringer than drugs. On a lecture circuit, he was wearing a white robe and beads. He had a beard and long hair, all part of his uniform of a new self found in a time apart in India. He describes the audience mostly also wearing their own uniforms of hippie dress. During the lecture, a woman of years, out of the uniform of the day, was simply sitting on the front row with her black comfort shoes and conservative dress. She had a knowing smile as Ram Dass described his many escapades in the drug culture before discovering the more satisfying, lasting effectives of meditation. Her nodding agreement raised doubt that she could possibly identify with what he was sharing. He began to wonder if the nodding were a physical part of her years of age or a sign she might have been feeling sleepy. When the lecture was over, his curiosity overtook him, and he questioned her about what she did that allowed her such understanding his experiences.

She replied, "Oh, I crochet."

All of these practices can result in baby steps of connecting with the wisdom within. The whole purpose of it all is to get on with our journey of maturing. As we each do our work of maturing, it nurtures a life that, because it was lived fully, leaves the world a better place.

KATE, THE SERVING SAGE

*A good head and a good heart
are always a formidable combination*[1].
Nelson Mandela

*I don't know what your destiny will be, but one thing
I know: Only the ones among you who will be truly
happy are those who have sought and found how to serve.*
Albert Schweitzer[2]

> Such a life, you are soon to discover, was lived by Kate Roos. Our mutual passion for peace brought Kate into my life. I admire her dedication to people in need of encouragement. She has the skill to give without taking away the receiver's dignity, nor their responsibility to be accountable for his or her own choices. All this seems to come naturally to her, without thought of the personal consequences some of her efforts might bring upon herself, which I find remarkable. Her adult son's request to hear more of her story began to open her eyes that she had led more than an ordinary life. He voiced his need to know more of the details of some risks she took that, as a child, he sensed more than understood. She said she told him her story in relation to her experiences of the God of her understanding that her early life formed.

I just did what any thinking, caring person would do. I don't think I am unusual in any way. Until recently, I certainly would not have seen my story as having any value worth recording. Then my son, whose life has been affected somewhat by the risks I took, called and asked if he could come see me and bring a tape recorder. He wanted to record an interview.

"I've come to recognize the courage with which you have lived your life," he said. "It has inspired mine, and I want to hear your whole story. When you sheltered the young man from Guatemala, I had a sense I was not supposed to tell any of my friends in school why Gustavo was living in our house. When they asked about him, I just made up stories without knowing the entire story myself. Now I'm ready to hear all of your story."

It all began when I was born. The guidance of my godparents (a wonderful term), who thought I needed to be part of a loving church family, provided my first relationship to God because my own earthly family was anything but loving. How fortunate for me that their own faith led them to pursue this on my behalf. Once everyone got through my christening and the rest of my infancy, I took on some responsibility for my own relationship with God, memorizing the Catholic catechism at St. Thomas Roman Catholic Church when I was five. It was like memorizing the alphabet, numbers, spelling rules, and favorite stories like *See Spot Run*, all useful endeavors that led to more autonomous and complex ones later in life.

Like school's mental chores and intellectual teachings, the catechism classes and First Unitarian Universalist Church I attended cemented a permanent bond to God. (My mother was Catholic; my father was Unitarian Universalist.) In those years, I was glad God loved me. (God was always a man in those days.) God's love was the last thing in the world I wanted to question. I thought it was just great. It never dawned on me in those early years that Catholics, Unitarians, and assorted other "isms" were different. I just thought God visited different kinds of churches every week but was the same God in all of them. Thankfully, I was too young and naïve to comprehend denominationalism.

Along the way, I soaked up concepts of mercy, forgiveness, kindness, truth, love, compassion, hope, integrity, peace, community, and justice. And all along the way, the concepts were obvious because they took shape in people I knew. Had they just been in the realm of great ideas, I probably would have dismissed them when I reached my teen years and thought Elvis Presley and

I. Leahanna Young

the twist were great ideas. But the reality of these concepts took root in the way I experienced them in extraordinary people. Love added a new substance to the cement that bound me to God. It was a living substance. For a while, I called it communion, the symbol of a living God. Then I began to refer to this substance as "role model" and "hero." Now I understand that God-in-relationship really is communion after all.

How do I know God? God is where love resides. I know God in my personal relationships, in Minnie Mae and Joseph, my grandparents. They were Mormons and led a life of service to others that was so strong that it affects me even to this day. It resides in Genevieve Johnson, a Quaker, mentor, and high school teacher. Her influence was profound enough that her love changed my life. I wish I had told her.

It resides in my parents, flawed and abusive as they were, in many ways, yet they believed each person had to choose his or her own God and led their kids to do just that. It resides in a college professor, a Quaker and pacifist, whose classes and teaching style showed what a belief in integrity was about.

Love resides in a counselor who asked me what I thought would make me happy. The next day, I drove four hours to see my father (whom I had not seen in twenty years) to tell him I forgave him for the abuse he had inflicted on his kids. Both of our lives were transformed as a result of that meeting. Later, when Dad and I were together with my siblings, someone suggested that we all tell about the person we now most admired. Simultaneously, I said "Dad," and he said "Kate."

Love resides in Father O'Shaughnessy, a Catholic priest and my partner in the sanctuary movement's Underground Railroad that brought Salvadoran and Guatemalan refugees (including Gustavo) from an Arizona border church to asylum in Canada.

It lives in Pat, another Quaker friend, with whom I worked on nuclear disarmament years ago. It lives in Leon Shenandoah, the Onondaga chief with whom I worked on a land dispute issue. He showed the world what simplicity meant by the way he lived and led his people. Love lives in Clyde Bullecourt, an American Indian

Movement leader with whom I had the great privilege of working following the siege at Wounded Knee. Everything about him spoke of forgiveness.

It lives in Sandra, my best childhood friend and Jew. She and her parents showed me what tolerance really meant. I was invited to their Seders and synagogue as if I were their daughter. It lives in Gita, an Iranian émigré, who is so grateful to God for everything.

It lives in Carolyn and Dan, Methodist pacifists whose lives were rich even though Dan gave up a lucrative job because it would have compromised his opposition to war. He then chose the richness of simple living and used his engineering skills for peace, including work on potable water projects in Central America.

Love resides in William Kunstler, a great lawyer, and lawyers from the Center for Constitutional Rights with whom I had the privilege of working as a volunteer for seven years on the Attica Brothers Prison project. Sixty men were helped through their work, including John Hill, a Mohawk Indian falsely charged with murder. Through their incredible commitment to justice, I saw God's hope and love. Love resides in the few who encouraged me to continue in a civil rights action I brought on behalf of Native Americans. I won the suit, but I paid what I thought was a huge cost in bringing the case. A more mature understanding of love reminds me that the cost I paid was not so bad. The cost paid by those who face injustice and have no one to stand up for them is inestimable.

I have been blessed to know God through these relationships. At last, I believe I get it. I understand God through what Henri Nouwen calls the Eucharistic life. It is in relationships that we know communion after all.

If I think I really know God though, I also know I'm in for a few more surprises before I'm gone. I have seen and known God in people of many different faiths, backgrounds, and cultures. I believe God is a mystery and so much larger than I am capable of understanding even through these limited (but blessed) experiences. To think I should have had relationships with such incredible people! Only God could give me that.

I. Leahanna Young

When I get a new book, I never read the last chapter first. I never want to know how it ends up until I get to the last page. I love a good mystery!

At one time in my history, when I had completed my degree, I experienced great difficulty in obtaining a teaching position. Finally, I was offered a job, but the offer was rescinded without explanation a week later. A couple years later, the mystery was cleared up when I was finally able to get a copy of my FBI files obtained with a Freedom of Information Act request. Incredibly and inaccurately, the information in the file listed me as a member of the American Indian Movement (regarded as a terrorist organization at that time). The information in the files, false as it was, had been shared with universities, including my own and two of the places where I had interviewed for a teaching job. Unable to find a teaching position, I took whatever was available, a job as a secretary during the day and cleaning toilets at night, so I could take care of my young son and myself.

I worked with many denominations to bring justice to the innocent. Once I was jailed for trespassing in a federal building. Three others and I had made several visits to see our congressman. After he had cancelled several appointments, the office assistant told us that once again he probably would not be able to meet with us, as it was nearly five in the afternoon.

They replied respectfully, "That's all right. We will just wait."

At that point, we were locked in the office, and shortly thereafter, a policeman came, arrested us, and took us downtown to be booked on trespass charges. At the hearing, the judge agreed to release all of us with a $250 fine each, a hardship for us to pay.

In the early 1990s, I was offered a good job that took me to Albany. The new job gave me enough income to buy a house. I felt called to move into the inner city, even though real estate agents discouraged that idea. At last, I found one on my own, bought it, and moved in.

It was a typical inner-city neighborhood. Prostitutes and drug dealers operated openly on my block. There was even an occasional drive-by shooting. I convinced two of my neighbors, Lucy and Frank (a recovering addict), that the neighborhood needed a block party to bring everyone together. Fliers were put on every door, inviting everyone with the stipulation that everyone had to bring something to eat.

Soon, I began to hear the knock-knock-knock on my door repeatedly. Neighbors were asking, "What am I supposed to bring?"

Some were assigned napkins; others were assigned potato salad, hamburger buns, and all the makings for a summer party. The whole block turned out, including the neighborhood cop. I discovered these macho drug dealers were really just young kids who didn't even know how to grill a hamburger. The party was a revelation. The barrier between us that our labels had created began to be torn down.

Also on the block were forty-two children, none who had a dad at his or her home. My next project became the First Street Storybook Club, a library of children's books I collected and distributed from the stoop in front of my house. I told each child that he or she had to have a library card and could take one book. When it was returned, they were required to tell me what the book was about before checking out the next one. Some of the kids worked up to reading ten books each week. Pride was written all over their faces.

Next, I rented a little apartment in my basement to a young man from a family with limited means. He was starting his freshman year in the local college and needed a safe, quiet place to study. I talked with him about the importance of hanging in there. I sensed that financial needs were pushing him out to earn money. Finally, I asked him, if I paid his tuition, if he would stay with it, keep up his grades, and get his degree. When he agreed, I used a small inheritance from my mother to pay his tuition. He kept his word, graduated, and went on to law school.

During this time, Charlie came into my life, we fell in love, and he asked me to marry him. I said yes with the understanding that we stay in my home in the inner city. Charlie had a job with a high security clearance, and his boss told him that he could not move into that neighborhood. Thankfully, he took the chance, and we were blessed that he did not in fact lose his job.

Charlie was as naïve as I was at first about living in this neighborhood. At times, I needed to help him understand how to live there safely. One of the drug dealers was also well known for his sweet potato pies, and Charlie wanted to try one. One day, he was gone longer than necessary. I went to find him. There he sat in the kitchen having a neighborly conversation with the pie maker (the drug dealer). Because police raids were not uncommon, I suggested it would be safer not to go inside to pick up any pies he bought in the future.

My many life experiences have given me a vision of a way to use the wisdom of elders, combined with the vitality and knowledge of the young, to co-create a better world.

What if we were willing to mix it up some? Instead of organizing committees, church activities, and government around age groups, we organized around themes such as those interested in working toward:

Peace

Justice

Economic improvement for all

Safe housing opportunities

Communication skills to facilitate greater intergenerational interaction

Respecting diversity

Henri Bergson reminds us, "The eye sees only what the mind is prepared to comprenhend"[3]

At the time of the interview, Kate was a member of the League of Women Voters and participating in local peace activities. She was also giving loving care to Charlie as together they dealt with the challenges of aging. Her most recent peace offering is a project she created called "Letters to my Sisters." The "Sisters" (all brought together by Kate) each write a monthly letter on topics as varied as "my favorite recipe" to "the most important person in my life." We sisters are a diverse family, including Christian, Bahai, Hindu, Islamic, and Buddhist faiths. Differing cultures are represented as well as age ranges. Most of us have never met. We send our letter monthly to Kate, who then compiles them into one email that everyone receives. At the end of this year, we hope to arrange a face-to-face potluck family dinner. Kate, by her life and word, believes living our faith in all its detail is the witness to peace to which we are called. You can see this in the topics the Sisters address, from the mundane to the big picture philosophical. All have importance and represent how each of us lives our faith. A mission for peace leaves no small thing unnoticed. Since the interview, Kate and Charlie have moved to be closer to family who could help with their care.

Kate reading to First Street Story Book Club

I. Leahanna Young

Kate & Lucy with First Street Story Book Club

COURAGE TO LIVE ON THE EDGE

... grow so that your mind is like a room with many open windows. Let the breeze flow in from all directions, but refuse to be blown away by any one.[1]
Arun Gandhi

Sages have a deep commitment to be always in line with an inner truth that outweighs their need for being accepted or to live in a life of comfort. This gives them the courage to step out, to go against common opinion, even when what many hold as common sense is recognized as untrue by wisdom. There is a sense they possess that goes beyond the common. Though these edge walkers appear ordinary in many ways, their extraordinary courage fuels them to stay true against odds under which many fold.

They go within themselves to listen for the highest truths. They may be great teachers, masters of art or science or leaders. In their legacy is a reference to a time of going apart from the crowds. When they come out from time apart, it is not to fight but to stand firm with deep compassion for all. We saw this in Gandhi, Nelson Mandela, Martin Luther King Jr., and many others.

Inner wisdom is a quieting force that meets all voices of fear from without and within. Fear does not mean wise ones are without fear. Rather, fear does not rule their actions. There is conversion of the power of fear or anger into thoughtful action that considers the welfare of all and the long-term consequence of a chosen action. It is seen as a strength that sustains in the face of threats and punishments of all kinds. Such threats empower rather than diminish their devotion to wisdom. The example of this use of empowerment inspires followers. It ignites and awakens what is known as our better angels. Certainly, it has been a force to be reckoned with, even feared and attacked, a force that has been known to result in real and lasting change.

Think of Gandhi's lasting challenge of, "Be the change you want to see in world. When ask for his parting words of wisdom, he tossed them from the train written on a brown paper bag. "My life is my message."[2]

Recall how Gandhi's example of courage to achieve major change through nonviolent action inspired Dr. Martin Luther King Jr. His message of "I have a dream" continues to bring changes of greater freedom for all. Dr. King's definition of courage is another legacy he left us. "Courage faces fear and thereby masters it."[3]

The movie *Invictus* demonstrated Mandela's courage to stand strong for his convictions in the lack of much agreement, even from his supporters. This inner sureness, perhaps formed partly from his humbling years of imprisonment continues to call us to tap into our own inner strength. He showed the world how working together instead of against each other can let both a sports team and a country find its way back into some unity. What an example Mandela gives the world of the hard-to-believe strength of resisting bitterness. Instead, he chose to make forgiveness rule his mind. Often history shows this is a measure of true greatness, not the weakness those of lesser vision taunt it as being.

There is a tendency to think of males when we hear the word "courage." I challenge you to consider the courageous females in your own life or history. Reading more of the lives of women such as Marie Curie, Helen Keller and her teacher Anne Sullivan, and Harriet Tubman will expand our automatic mind response when we hear "courage," a word of such power.

A woman of courage I came to admire through my work at Heart of the Hills Hospice in the hill country of Texas is Elizabeth Kubler Ross. Elizabeth claimed her own identity apart from being one of triplets. She recounts that, when sometimes sitting on her father's lap, she knew he didn't know which of the three she was. They were dressed alike and usually given an average C grade if one performed exceptionally well and one poorly, as even the teachers couldn't tell them apart. The fact that she took her studies to the level of becoming a medical doctor tells me she was likely the one doing well.

She devoted much of her life to the study of death and dying. Through her work, she has taught those ready to learn much about living. In 1995, she had a paralyzing stroke. At first, she assumed it was time to apply all her life's learning to this time of her own dying. Surprisingly, she found what she needed to access was her courage to continue to live in and teach from a paralyzed body. In *Life Lessons*, Elizabeth and co-author, David Kessler, end-of-life specialist, teach us about the mysteries of life and living.[4]

Living on the edge with courage and higher wisdom requires introspection. This principle is one distinction between what we identify as worldly heroes and wise ones. Those who act on earthly commands, a burst of adrenalin or self-serving motives, may be seen as heroes, but history tends to fade their glory. Time is kind to the wise. Even if their courage results in the death of their body, their ideas and truth grow stronger as time passes. It also separates the wise ones from the know-it-alls who never dare to go within or question their own present knowing.

It is an interesting study to notice how this practice of gathered courage leads to an appearance of lightness and humor. It may have been the motivation for the Dalai Lama to write a book on the art of happiness. It is easy to see the nearly mischievous twinkle in his eye as he answers questions spontaneously from a group of people or an interviewer. Inner joy and knowing shines forth from him that makes time in his presence a delight. It echoes with curiosity of "What is next?" That quality of curiosity is an essential element of all sages.

It would be wise for us to set it free in ourselves as an aid to our journey.

Once, my little girl self was out for an adventure across town with Lahoma. We were best friends and, in our minds, daring adventurers. On this day, we met a man who warned us, "You girls better take your doll buggies and head home now. Lavelle is out looking for you with her switch."

In fact, this happened not once, but several times. We wandered out of our neighborhood to explore the larger world. Though we thought of it as exploring, my mother, Lavelle, saw it differently and came looking for us time and again to switch us all the way home. We longed to find answers to those questions in our young minds, "What is out beyond where we are? What else is there we haven't yet seen or experienced?"

Living in the small town where we had such a sense of safety is a treasured part of my history. That little girl, explorer and wanderer, remains alive and well, living in a body that has explored places, ideas, people, and experiences that brought unspeakable joy and agonizing pain. Now I see how those adventures and experiences have made me stretch and grow. I find myself in my eighth decade of life, that period Gail Sheehy refers to as the "Sage Seventies" in her book, *The New Passages*[5]

In *The Art of Aging*, Sherwin B. Nuland, clinical professor of surgery at Yale University, describes the remarkable life of Michael E. DeBakey, the famous heart surgeon. Dr. DeBakey explains, "It is this aspect of seeking knowledge . . . curiosity; curiosity is a transcendent life force."[6]

I find the more I allow curiosity to lead me to explore, the less I fear. The less I fear, the more freedom I enjoy. The freer I feel, the richer my life and the more interesting the people I invite in to participate in my freedom. It seems freedom is contagious. It is not something I have fought for or earned. It is simply experienced in the midst of whatever circumstance I find myself. Knowing I always have choices keeps me free in spirit.

Jean, Sage of Many Learnings

Don't be backward about going forward!
Lowell Collins, Sage Jean's art teacher

> A sage who has the courage to live on the edge is Jean Murray. If you did not know Jean well, you might not see the strength she demonstrates. People, who fail to recognize this strength, can be surprised by it, even offended or embarrassed by it. Underneath her gentle, slender appearance, there is the strength of steel. She often taught Tai Chi as the graceful dancelike martial art form it can be. She, in fact, often played music as we went through the form—sometimes Andrea Bocelli, the Italian opera singer, or maybe country and western, depending on which part of the form she was emphasizing at the time. Her movements were always graceful, even when she switched to the defensive martial arts practice of Tai Chi. She expected her students to be attentive and allowed no slackness. She could come across with a tone of voice that some saw as rough. Those who knew her well knew it came from her devotion to the practice and an expectation that respect be practiced as well. The respect she demanded included self-respect. The words "sorry, sorry" heard from beginners who found themselves facing the wrong direction were quickly replaced by Jean to "oops." Her view was dedicated students do not make mistakes, only opportunities for new learning. She commanded the respect her students showed her because of the dedicated and competent teacher she always showed up as being.

A sage of great influence in my life was Mr. Lowell Collins. He was an artist and gallery owner. He was connected with the Museum School of Art in Houston. He was owner of his own school of art, an appraiser, an international expert in Pre-Colombian art, and a father. He taught me to paint and see more clearly and how to teach. I'll explain.

"Don't be backward about going forward!" he'd encourage when a student bogged down on a painting or life.

"You can't make candy out of dirt!" he'd admonish if someone tried to use poor materials or bad technique.

"That little area right there is a jewel," Lowell would say, pointing to a small, specific place on my canvas. And later again, he'd say, "That little area is a jewel," as he pointed to another place.

Then he'd go to read his mail or pay bills until it was time for another round. "Solve the corners and the middle," he'd say to those struggling with composition.

He never painted on any student's canvas. He might not speak to any of us for an hour until someone needed the encouragement of, "Don't be backward about going forward."

"The jewels," he explained to me, "will add up to a masterpiece."

His job was showing us when something was a jewel. Eventually, everything we painted would become a jewel, a masterpiece. He didn't critique as so many art teachers do. About as heavy as it ever got with Lowell was the day he kept telling one of my fellow painters, "That's too much green." He kept it up all day.

At the end of the day, he came over to me and said, "Darn it, Jean, that is too much yellow."

I was startled as he hadn't said one word to me directly that day. The question I felt must have shown on my face.

He laughed. "Jean, you learn best by listening and observing what goes on around you. You're a peripheral learner. If I want you to know something, I tell another student."

Lowell's lessons stand me in good stead for the challenges of my life. Afraid to teach Tai Chi? "Don't be backward about going forward." Learn to drive at fifty? "Solve the corners and the middle. You can't make candy out of dirt." And while teaching, I would see, "That little area right there is a jewel." Lowell Collins was a treasure, a master teacher.

Elena Brineman was to become my Tia Elena, my family by choice. Elena traveled the world with her husband, Jack, as he looked for oil as a geologist. She lived in Venezuela, Guatemala, Canada, and Iran. She spent her childhood in Cuba, and she was fluent in Spanish and English. She could speak French and learned Farsi. I worked for her as her Girl Friday at her home travel business. She taught by example. She was always courteous, kind, and happy to meet someone. She was no respecter of class. She cherished all who came into her path. She listened. That was perhaps her greatest gift. She also taught. If people were unwilling to take on a public project that she knew needed doing, she'd read them the story of "The Little Red Hen." Who among them wanted to be one of those who wanted the bread without being willing to work for it? No one did, and a lot of folks stepped up to the plate after those readings.

All the years I knew and cherished Elena's friendship, she let me do things. She let me help in the kitchen. She let me put away the *nacimiento*, a big collection of small figures from Central and South America used to make nativity scenes. I'd be knee deep in some tasks before it would dawn on me that Elena had let me do something again. I'd find myself laughing and enjoying the task more.

She also taught me, "Jean, be mad when you are mad instead of hurt."

I was glad she let me be her friend, her family by choice. It was an honor.

Sifu Dr. Clay Cox came into my life as the result of an asking meditation I did twice where I asked for my master teacher. I asked twice and received two teachers, Sifu Cox and Sifu Steven Kronnick. With that meditation, they both began to look for me. And they showed up in my art class at Lowell's even though I wasn't fully aware of that at the time. I did two paintings. One was of a child. One was of a redheaded man with freckles. I was so annoyed by it that I painted over it with what I thought, at the time, was a portrait of a young girl. The redheaded man was Sifu Dr. Clay Cox. The child was Sifu Steven Kronnick. This was years before I met either of them in person.

I. Leahanna Young

Sifu Steven taught with a quiet love. When I behaved poorly, he whispered in my ear, "Fuck you very much." It was said without an iota of rancor or anger.

Steven was on a mission from the moment I walked into his presence. He knew he didn't have much time. He began teaching me Tai Chi form and then how to teach form. He gave me a student and asked me to teach her a short portion of the Tai Chi form. I had to ask him to show me that part. He did. Then he kept his eye on me as I taught, but he did not interfere. He taught me a lot about listening. He said of me after my first class, "Not a beginner." He reminded me of our love for one another beyond this lifetime and gave me a portrait, an old print, "of us in another life." He's still my teacher and guide, even though he is no longer in a physical body.

Dr. Cox came to me in person on the occasion of Steven's death. He stayed in my home for about a week. What he lived in front of my eyes was grace. He was Steven's foster father and had known him over twenty years. He spoke softly. He asked questions. And yet, in the midst of great sorrow as Steven's death was a mystery, a murder, he paid attention to my needs and concerns. He laughed with me and wept when he needed to weep. He turned Steven's Tibetan meditation bowl upside down on my head and laughed when he rang it.

Dr. Cox knew I was grieving not only Steven's death but also my sister's. He quietly comforted me. "I want you to stay on the form, Ms. Jean. Okay?"

Okay. All these years he has quietly encouraged me, taught me, and loved me when I didn't think I was lovable. He taught me that, for him, Tai Chi was "the breath I found along the Way." He also admonished, "Read the Tao. Read the Tao. Read the Tao." He gave me the four principles of Tai Chi:

- Love the deity.
- Accept divine providence.
- Don't interfere.
- No. No. No. Just have fun.

William David Kirk, also known as "Brother," was my cousin who suffered brain damage during his birth. I think only old souls serve us in these roles. He taught me compassion. His mother, my Aunt Lilly, explained to me that Brother couldn't do all the things I could do. He couldn't wash or dress himself or speak to me. He could hear me. They thought he was blind. When Brother's state was explained to me, I was about six years old. One fine day, he and his parents came to visit. I remembered Brother needed help doing even small things, but as a child, that didn't so much matter as the fact I had a playmate for the afternoon. I led him around the yard and orchard and learned he would follow my voice. I showed him my pepper plants. He smiled and smelled them. Wow! He followed me back to the house and climbed the steps all by himself. A first! This way, the adults learned that he could see. He became too big for my aunt and uncle to care for and manage at home. He lived out his life in a state home. He loved music and would sometimes sing, "You Are My Sunshine." He was always sunshine in my life for the lessons he brought me as a young child.

So many other influences are worth mentioning. My daddy said, "Walk in another man's moccasins before you judge him." And he lifted up the fresh-plowed dirt in his farmer's hands and said to me, "This is Mother Earth. Be kind to Her, and She will be kind to you." His name was Charles Alfred Stewart.

And my mother nudged me one day late in her life. "Come here. I want to show you something. See those trees across the alley?" I did. "Just look at them now! That's how trees are." The trees had been pruned back severely but were growing past their wounds and all attempts to control them. My mother's name was Anna Mae Stewart, nee Sawyer.

There are more, but these were the best of the best.

Benjamin Hoff wrote, "Lots of people talk to animals,' said Pooh. 'Not that many listen though. That's the problem.'"[1]

Afterword

Here is the possibility for a new beginning of your journey. As you use the ABCs and other resources of *Savoring Sage Time*, you can open your own account to deposit new treasures for your ongoing journey.

Are you one of the humble ones that can't imagine yourself as a sage? Wake up! If you have unfinished dance steps to learn, get to dancing. See yourself in some of these sage stories or perhaps your own unique story still writing itself as you peel away the layers that have been hiding it.

Know that everyone has a story to tell. If he or she has done the work of growing through completing the tasks of each decade of his or her lives and has lived at least eight decades, he or she probably has stories filled with the wisdom of experience just waiting to be told to a willing ear. All that is needed from the listening ear is to hear without judgment or any need to fix or alter his or her story for the listener's comfort. Breathe through any discomfort the painful parts of the story bring. Remember, the pain honestly experienced by one fully present is part of the crucible of fire through which sages courageously walk. If there are tears, be present to them. If there is laughter, open your heart to its contagion. If there is readiness for celebration, joyfully join it. It is often helpful to state specifically any inspiration you feel when the story is finished. For example, "When you told of the time you . . . I was inspired to . . ."

I count as sacred privilege the stories I have heard and recounted here for you. May you be so blessed as you become the willing listener to the sages in your life.

I. Leahanna Young

I Choose to Make
The Rest of my Life
The Best of my Life[1]

Louise Hay

Will you join Louise and me in our choice?

ENDNOTES

Preface
1. Arun Gandhi, *A Legacy of Love: My Education in the Path of Nonviolence* (El Sobrante, CA: North Bay Books, 2003), 136.
2. Joan Chitterster, *The Gift of Years* (New York: Blue Ridge, 2001), 55.

Introduction
1. Emily Dickinson, www.iwise.com/j0G5Y.
2. Martin Buber, www.brainyquote.com/authors/m/martin_buber.html.
3. *Mrs. Delafield Wants to Marry* (2005 KOC Galaxy Productions).

Accept Gifts of the Sage
1. Henry David Thoreau, www.everyday-wisdom.com/wisdom-quotes.html.
2. Random House Webster's College Dictionary, (New York, NY: Random House, Inc.,1992) 1183
3. Joan Chittister, *The Gift of Years*, 127;
4. Doug Meckelson and Diane Haithman, *Elder Wisdom Circle Guide for a Meaningful Life* (London: PLUME, Penguin Group), 253.
5. Barry Barkan, "Culture of Change in Long-Term Care, Part I," *Journal of Social Work in Long-Term Care* 2 ½ (2003): 201.
6. William H. Thomas M.D.,What are Old People For How Elders Will Save the World,(Acton, Massachusetts: Vanderwick & Burham, 2007) 105

I. Leahanna Young

Time as Treasure
1. Cicero, www.brainyquotes.com.
2. Joseph Campbell,goodreads.com/quotes/5300-where-you-stumble-and-fall-there-you-will-find-gold
3. Cicero quote from Joan Chittister, *The Gift of Years*, 12
4. Pablo Picasso, www.Wordreference a Language Forum.

Dorothy, Astrological Sage
1. William Wordsworth, www.iwise.com/a USA

Accumulate Graces on Flights in Time
1. Jimmy Carter, *The Virtues of Aging* (Henderson, TN: Ballentine Press, 1998), 73.

Get Right Side Up from Upside Down
1. Confucius, www.thinkexist.com.
2. Richard Rohr, *Falling Upward* (San Francisco: Josey-Bass, 2011), 151.
3. www.pbs.org/wgbh/nova/physics/theory-of-everything.html.
4. Eckhart Tolle, "On Happiness" www.coyoteprime-runningcausecantfly.blogspot.com.January 12,2010.
5. Martha's Blog, "Aliveness," www.marthaobrien.com, August 2, 2012.

Arthur, the Bounce-Back Sage
1. www.cleanandsobernotdead.com.
2. Winston Churchill, www.brainyquotes.com/authors/w/Winston_churchill.html.

The Blocks to Maturity
1. Susan Howatch, The Starbridge Series, Glittering Images, (G.K. Hall Large Print Book Series 1987)
2. Richard Rohr, *A Spirituality for the Two Halves of Life Lectures*

Living an Attitude of Gratitude

1. Marcel Proust, www.quotationspage.com/quote/31288.html.
2. Mahatma Gandhi, www.quotationspage.com/quote/27184.html.
3. Eckhart Tolle, The Power of Now A Guide to Spiritual Enlightment, (Novato,CA, New World Library) 1999
4. William H. Thomas, *What are Old People For? How Elders Will Change the World* (Acton, MA: Van Wyk & Burham, 2004).
5. Elizabeth Kubler-Ross and David Kessler, *Life Lessons* (New York: Scribner, 2000), 15,
6. Virginia Ironside, *You're Old, I'm Old . . . Get Used to It! 20 Reasons Why Growing Old Is Great* (New York: Viking Penguin Group, 2009), 175.

Build Balance into Life

1. Socrates, www.brainyquote.com/quotes/quotes/s/Socrates133712.html.
2. O.A. Battista, www.quoteworld.org/quotes/1066.

Enjoy the Mystery of Life's Journey

1. Richard Rohr, *The Naked Now* (Crossroads Publishing, 2009), 116.
2. Charles Filmore, *Mysteries of John*, 13th edition (Unity Village, MO: Unity School of Christianity, 1949), 13.

Critique the Critic

1. Rex Sikes, http://idea-seminars.com/articles/affirm.htm
2. Henriette Anne Klauser, *Writing on Both Sides of the Brain (San Francisco, CA Harper & Row1986)* 77

Vicki, Learner Sage
1. Paula Underwood, *Recorder of Oral Stories, The Walking People* (San Anselmo, CA: A Tribe of Two Press, 1993).
2. Eleanor Roosevelt, http://stumblingtowardhealth.wordpress.com/2011/05/20/you-must-do-the-thing-you-think-you-cannot-do-eleanor-roosevelt/
3. General George Patton (also attributed to Andrew Jackson), http://marshianchronicles.com/?p=119
4. Marshall Rosenberg, *Nonviolent Communication: A Language of Life* (Encinitas, CA: Puddledance Press Book, 2003), 21.

Sage or Sourpuss, Your Choice: Using Our Power to Choose
1. Tom Robbins, www.thinkexist.com/we-are-our-own-dragons-as-well-aspheroes/357307.html.
2. Art Linklletter, www.quoteworld.org/quotes/8370.
3. Doug Meckelson and Diane Haithmore, *The Elder Wisdom Circle Guide for Meaningful Life* (New York: Plume Book, Penguin Press, 2007), 253.

Martin "Old Eagle" Native Wisdom Sage
1. Jamie Sams and Carson, David, *Medicine Cards* (New York, N.Y., St. Martin's Press 1999) 41
2. Native Legend, *Two Hungry Wolves,* httP://www.tumblr.com/tagged-two-wolves?before+13330179905

Segue into Sage: Avoid Slip into Senility
1. Vivian Green, http://letmetypeitout.wordpress.com/2012/09/03 danceinrain.
2. William Arthur Ward, http://thinkexist.com/quotations/forgiveness_is_a_funny_thing_it_warms_the_heart/8446.html.
3. "Hong Kong's Secrets to Longevity," www.newsmaxhealth.com, August 31, 2012.

4. Ram Dass, Collector's Edition CD on Conscious Aging (Boulder, CO: Audio Publishing Event Sounds True, 2000).
5. Chris Crowley and Lodge, MD Henry S., *Younger Next Year Live Strong, Fit, and Sexy: Until You're 80 and Beyond* (New York: Workman, 2004), 29.
6. Senile medical definition: http://www.medterms.com/script/main/art.asp?articlekey=33489
7. Gary Small, MD, *Alzheimer's Prevention Program* (New York: Workman Publishing Company), 2011.

Sages in Disguise
1. Harrison Ford, www.quotesdaddy.com/author/Harrison/Ford.
2. Biblical Quote: Hebrews 6:13:2, New International Version (Grand Rapids, MI, Zondervan Bible Publishers 1984) 896

Smokey, Sage on a Motorcycle
1. Martin Fischer, http://thinkexist.com/quotations/knowledge-is-a-process-of-piling-facts-wisdom/215858.html.
2. William Jennings Bryan, http://quoteworld.org/2011.

Connect with Change: The Twain Can Meet
1. James Harvey Robinson, http://quoteworld.org/quotes/2011.
2. Tom Robbins, http:thinkexist.com/quotes/tom_robbins.

Nancy, the Teaching Sage
1. Robert Fulghum, http:www.cof.edu/Resources/VOICE/instructorlessonplans/personaldevelop/missionstatement/mstatement2/text/pdf.

Wisdom of Full Presence
1. Marianne Williams, *Everyday Grace* (New York: Riverhead Books, 2002).
2. Pema Chödron, *The Wisdom of No Escape and the Path of Loving Kindness* (London and Boston: Shambala, 1991).

Kate, the Serving Sage
1. Nelson Mandala, http://www.quotes.net/3126.
2. Albert Schweitzer, http://en.proverbia.net/citasautor.asp?autor=16543
3. Henri Bergson, http://thinkexist.com/quotation/the_eye_sees_only_what_the_mind_is _prepared_to/13601.html.

Courage to Live on the Edge
1. Arun Gandhi, *Legacy of Love, My Education in the Path of Nonviolence* (El Sobrante, CA: Noah Bay Books, 2003)
2. Mahatma Gandhi, http://www.thinkexist.com/mahatma_gandhi.
3. Dr. Martin Luther King http://www.brainyquotes/quotes/author/n/martin_luther_king_1_4html.
4. Elizabeth Kubler-Ross and David Kessler, *Life Lessons* (New York: Scribner, 2000)
5. Gail Sheehy, New Passages Mapping Your Life Across Time,(New York, Ballantine Books,1995) 424
6. Sherwin B. Nuland, *The Art of Aging* (New York: Random House, 2008).

Jean, Sage of Many Learnings
1. Benjamin Hoff, *The Tao of Pooh* (London: Penguin Books, 1994).
2. Afterword
3. Louise Hay, www.thequotefactory.com/quotes-by/louise_hay_/i-choose-to-make-the-rest-of45358.